AF632819

Energy-efficient Computing for Modern AI Applications

Verses Kindler Publication

Verses Kindler Publication.

Website: www.verseskindlerpublication.com

Energy-efficient Computing for Modern AI Applications

By: Mr. Bhanu Prakash Reddy Rella and

Mr. Sujit Reddy Thumma

ISBN: 978-93-49532-72-4

1st Edition

Price: INR 349/$18

Disclaimer

Energy-efficient Computing for Modern AI Applications is authored by Bhanu Prakash Reddy Rella and Sujit Reddy Thumma. The entirety of this published work comprises the original content of the author, who has undertaken diligent efforts in its editing. The characters depicted herein may be fictitious or inspired by real events; however, they are not intended to cause offense or represent any prejudice against any caste or system. Any similarity to the names of actual individuals, locations, or institutions is purely coincidental and serves the narrative. The author bears sole responsibility for the originality of this work; the publisher assumes no liability thereof.

Index

Chapter 1: Introduction to Energy-Efficient AI

The Rising Demand for AI and Its Energy Implications

Artificial intelligence (AI) is essentially the ability of machines to mimic cognitive functions that were previously thought to be unique to humans, such as information acquisition, problem solving, and decision making. Models based on deep learning, particularly neural networks, and large language models (LLMs) are two of the most potent forms of artificial intelligence. These models use enormous amounts of computing power to identify patterns in massive datasets and generate wise predictions or judgements.

However, there are substantial drawbacks associated with this wonderful potential, particularly when it comes to energy usage. Modern AI systems need a lot of processing power for both inference (the ongoing use of these algorithms to make content, make predictions, or talk to users) and the building blocks of complex models. AI's energy footprint is increased by this dual necessity, raising questions about sustainability, the influence on the environment, and economic viability.

AI's Power-Hungry Nature: A Look at Large Models

Large neural networks, particularly large language models, are a major component of the AI world of today. Some significantly popular ones are as follows: Meta: LLaMA (Large Language Model Meta AI), Google: BERT (Bidirectional Encoder Representations from Transformers), along with OpenAI: GPT series (Generative Pre-trained Transformers). The AI model adjusts these massive models' billions or even trillions of parameters during training to improve performance.

Take OpenAI's GPT-3, one of the largest and most significant large language models ever created, to understand the scope. During training, GPT-3 used a projected 1,287 megawatt-hours (MWh) of power with about 175 billion parameters. For comparison, 1,287 MWh of electrical energy is sufficient for running hundreds of typical American houses for a year. This enormous usage reveals a larger pattern: AI models are using more and more computing power, straining the capabilities of current infrastructure.

The Energy Coin's Two Sides: Training and Inference

Inference—using models that are trained to generate predictions or responses—consumes energy continuously over the model's operational lifetime, representing a significant ongoing demand, even though training these models makes headlines due to their astounding computation magnitude and corresponding energy demands. In reality, inference tasks as a whole use substantially more power over the initial training phase, even though they are less well acknowledged. This is because inference happens continually as millions or billions of users engage with AI-driven services on a daily basis, whereas model training is a single, albeit resource-intensive, occurrence.

Take ChatGPT as an example. Every subsequent inquiry that users worldwide submit to ChatGPT requires inference, using computational resources dispersed over numerous servers worldwide, after OpenAI's energy-intensive training of the original GPT models. The hidden but significant contributor to AI's general consumption of energy is inference, whose energy demands can potentially exceed the initial training footprint due to billions of interactions each month.

In actuality, a sizable amount of a company's operating energy expenses are attributed to inference jobs taken together. This continuous operational energy demand is significant and is fueled by AI models used in practical applications. Services that run constantly, like Netflix's real-time engine for recommendations, Facebook and Instagram's personalised feeds, and advanced predictive analytics in the financial or medical industries, gradually increase energy usage.

Examples of AI's Extreme Energy Requirements in the Real World

AI's growing energy requirements are glaringly evident in real-world implementations. Leading AI innovators, tech behemoths frequently release data highlighting their high energy consumption. With 175 billion parameters, OpenAI's GPT-3 required enormous amounts of energy for training, and it also needs more power for each interaction it performs. Similar to this, Google's DeepMind AlphaFold, an AI that can forecast protein shapes, required a large amount of processing power, thousands of GPU hours during training. Despite being innovative, these AI systems set the stage for ever more ambitious and thus more energy-demanding future models.

This energy consumption is also evident in specialised businesses outside of large IT companies. Because they must constantly collect and analyse sensor data, autonomous cars require a lot of processing power for things like real-time object recognition and decision-making algorithms. Examples of companies where continuous inference significantly raises energy costs are Tesla, Waymo, and Cruise. This is because these companies must analyze safety-critical autonomous vehicle choices around the clock.

Additionally, because of their decision-making algorithms and continuous, high-speed market information processing, AI-enabled securities trading systems utilised by international investment banks and hedge fund companies require enormous amounts of computational power. The financial industry's fierce quest for competitive advantages has been a major factor in the expansion of data centres and the increase in energy costs.

Why is AI So Power-Hungry?

Examining AI's computational nature is necessary to comprehend its enormous energy requirements. The majority of contemporary AI applications rely on neural networks, which require billions of floating-point calculations per second to run across several processor units. Because deep learning methods demand parallel processing, these processors, which are mostly GPUs (Graphics Processing Units), TPUs (Tensor Processing Units), or specialised AI accelerators, consume electricity at extraordinary rates.

The mathematical processes that underlie artificial intelligence are a major cause of its high power consumption. Especially during training, when a model iteratively processes enormous datasets, training from every instance, deep learning significantly relies on matrix multiplications and intricate computations. The attention techniques used by GPT-like transformer models, for example, greatly raise the computational and power needs as modelling sizes grow exponentially.

Furthermore, although inference tasks are usually easier than training tasks, they still require repetitive calculations. Around the world, these inference operations take place billions of times every day, adding to the cumulatively massive but less obvious energy use. The power consumed by continuous AI operations is steadily increasing as a result of customer expectations for instant, personalised outcomes from AI-powered assistants like Siri or Alexa, viewing suggestions from Netflix or Spotify, as well as personalised news feeds.

Factors Driving High AI Energy Consumption

Several critical factors intensify AI's energy demands:

- Model Size and Complexity: Typically, an enormous boost in processing power is needed for every small improvement in model complexity and accuracy. A neural network's scaling usually entails exponentially larger parameter numbers, which increases computational intensity and memory consumption.

- Data Processing and Movement: Frequent data transfers between memory, storage devices, and processors are necessary for data-intensive AI systems; each transfer has an energy cost. Specifically, data transfer and memory operations can account for more energy use than even computation expenses. This becomes especially evident in use cases requiring enormous computational resources, such as vision processing tasks (e.g., real-time image and video analysis, facial recognition, and augmented reality), where large volumes of data must be rapidly moved, processed, and interpreted, further amplifying overall energy consumption.

- Cooling and Infrastructure Overhead: Significant cooling infrastructure is needed in data centres that house AI workloads in order to handle the extreme heat produced by closely spaced, always-running technology. Overheads for power management and cooling can occasionally be more than the power consumed for computation itself.

Consequences of Unchecked Growth in AI Energy Consumption

The continued unchecked growth in AI's power demands poses several severe consequences, including:

- Environmental Concerns: Climate change is getting worse due to the growing reliance on data centres that are primarily run on fossil fuels. Although multiple tech giants have started switching to renewable energy, data centre growth is far exceeding the switch to renewable energy.

- Economic Pressure on Businesses: AI-driven expenses for energy are taking up more and more capacity in organisational budgets, which limits the amount of capital that can be spent on R&D, innovation, and other significant projects. Smaller businesses may find it difficult to use the latest AI technologies as the costs inflate, limiting innovation to those with strong financial support and a background.

Exponential Growth in AI Compute Demands

Over the past ten years, artificial intelligence has rapidly changed, especially in the form of deep neural networks and large language models (LLMs). Unprecedented advancements have been made throughout this time, with inventions stretching the limits of computational feasibility. Modern AI systems offer amazing capabilities, but they come at a high computational cost. The rise in processing power needed to create advanced AI has greatly surpassed past patterns, such as the well-known Moore's Law, in recent years. Moore's Law anticipated that the number of transistors on integrated circuits would approximately double every two years. But the computational demands of AI are increasing far more quickly than the advancements made possible by conventional semiconductor scaling.

The rate at which model sizes and, consequently, their computational complexity have increased is one key indicator to measure this sharp increase. Moore's Law has historically caused computer capacity to double around every two years, whereas AI's processing requirements now typically double every 3-4 months. Indeed, recent studies show that in just six years, the computing demands of state-of-the-art AI models have skyrocketed by an astounding factor of roughly 300,000 times. As the growth of AI is significantly quicker than Moore's Law, developmental concerns in the field of AI are prominent.

By today's standards, the initial GPT model, which was first presented in 2018, required a substantial amount of computational power and had about 117 million parameters. A year later, GPT-2 had grown significantly, with 1.5 billion parameters, more than 10 times the computing load. With its astounding 175 billion parameters, GPT-3, which was published in 2020, represented yet another enormous increase in resource requirements. By 2023, GPT-4 had advanced even further, outperforming its predecessors several orders of magnitude and requiring massive clusters of powerful GPUs to run nonstop for several weeks or months at a time. Numerically, over the last six years, the amount of computing power needed for AI has increased by about 300,000 times, far beyond any scaling trends that have been previously noted.

Beyond merely technological viability, this increasing trend poses important questions about the supply of energy, sustainable development, and financial sustainability. The worldwide energy footprint has increased as a result of cloud providers like Amazon AWS, Microsoft Azure, and Google Cloud constantly expanding their infrastructure to handle this exponential expansion. These companies now house enormous data centres built to satisfy AI's ravenous demand for processing capacity. The search for effective, sustainable AI solutions is not only desired, but also necessary because such exponential scale, if not handled responsibly, may put significant pressure on the world's energy supplies and magnify environmental effects.

Environmental Impact of Energy Consumption by AI

The swift growth and widespread application of artificial intelligence technologies, particularly the massive computing resources required to develop and operate these powerful models, directly lead to increased energy consumption and substantial greenhouse gas emissions. The importance of examining and addressing AI's role in the growing climate crisis is highlighted by the growing concern of the IT industry and the general public about this environmental impact.

Carbon Footprint of AI Training

To train a state-of-the-art AI model, complex computational processes are needed, typically performed on specialist hardware such as Graphics Processing Units (GPUs), Tensor Processing Units (TPUs), and Field-Programmable Gate Arrays (FPGAs). Carbon dioxide emissions are directly caused by these processes' high electricity consumption, especially when they are performed on an enormous scale. The extent of these emissions is demonstrated by the training of massive transformer-based language models, such as GPT-3. According to recent reports, the 284 metric tonnes of CO2 emitted during training were nearly equal to the emissions of five gasoline-powered passenger automobiles over their whole lifespan. These startling numbers paint a vivid picture of AI's growing climatic effects, demonstrating how carbon footprints rise quickly in tandem with processing needs.

Even while GPT-3 has a significant influence already, these effects are further made worse by the push towards ever-larger models. In comparison to previous generations, upcoming state-of-the-art models now have trillions of parameters, marking yet another quantum increase in processing resources and, consequently, emissions. As model sophistication increases, carbon emissions rise to previously unheard-of levels, prompting concerns about the sustainability and environmental effects of further AI development in the absence of major efficiency gains or the use of renewable energy sources.

Data Centers: Powerhouses with a Growing Environmental Cost

Data centres, which are sizable structures with numerous computers, storage areas, networking hardware, and cooling systems, are at the core of AI's energy issue. Nearly all operations, from training intricate models to making millions of real-time deductions every second worldwide, are supported by these data centres.

Data centres require a range of energy sources, including direct electricity for computations and indirect energy primarily from cooling and power distribution systems. Due to their intensive, continuous computational processes, GPUs, TPUs, and other specialised hardware frequently employed for AI activities generate a lot of heat. The requirement for big cooling systems significantly increases the indirect carbon footprint.

AI is also directly linked to higher greenhouse gas emissions because many data centres worldwide still rely on electricity produced from fossil fuels. Even if major players like GCP, Azure, and AWS are taking significant strides for data centres to be fuelled by renewable energy, the sheer scale and rapidity of development make a complete transition to environmentally friendly energy sources difficult.

Cooling Infrastructure: AI's Indirect Energy Burden

The need for advanced cooling technologies in data centres is a significant—yet sometimes disregarded—factor that increases AI's environmental impact. Examples of strong processors that produce considerable amounts of heat when running constantly at their full potential are GPUs and TPUs. Effective cooling systems are necessary to avoid overheating and guarantee the effectiveness of hardware.

However, because traditional cooling systems need a lot of electricity, data centres have far greater overall energy requirements. The ecological burden of cooling such power-hungry computational cores is rising.

Case Study: Google's AI for Data Center Energy Optimization

Interestingly, AI itself can be employed as part of the solution to regulate its environmental impacts in a paradoxical duality. Google's application of Artificial intelligence to increase the electricity efficiency of its cooling tech is a well-known illustration of this phenomenon. By employing deep learning algorithms to assess past operational data and accurately forecast cooling requirements in real time, they were able to cut the consumption of energy in their data centres by a staggering 40 percent.

AI should be utilised in conjunction with more all-encompassing sustainability measures, like the use of renewable energy sources, more energy-efficient hardware, and well-optimized software architectures that take energy usage into account, to improve energy efficiency.

Geo-distributed Training and Renewable Energy Strategies

Another possible approach to reduce the environmental impact of artificial intelligence is the deliberate use of geo-distributed development, which spreads workloads among geographically scattered data centres located in places abundant in green energy sources. Companies can greatly reduce their dependency on power produced from fossil fuels, therefore reducing their total environmental impact.

Data centers operated on environmentally benign sources include hydroelectric electricity, geothermal, and wind energy, sending vast amounts of processing loads. The cost of infrastructure, issues with synchronization and latency in distributed networks, and the unpredictability of clean energy sources are some of the practical barriers that stand in the way of this promising concept.

Furthermore, not every area with renewable resources has the connectivity, digital infrastructure, or political stability needed for widespread AI implementation. As a result, geo-distributed AI inference and training continue to be promising but incomplete answers to a challenging, multidimensional sustainability issue. Companies have to integrate these geo-distributed techniques with aggressive adoption of renewable energy, infrastructure-wide efficiency improvements, and broader societal measures to reduce climate impacts to get the best results.

Beyond Carbon: Broader Environmental Implications

AI's effects on the environment go beyond energy use and carbon emissions to include resource depletion and the production of electronic garbage. When exposed to huge workloads, GPUs, TPUs, and specialized AI accelerators have limited operational lifespans. Due to more frequent replacement cycles brought on by this accelerated hardware obsolescence, significant e-waste streams are produced, and the depletion of vital resources like rare earth metals and minerals is hastened.

Specialized AI hardware component production and disposal have significant environmental impacts as well, involving risky chemical exposure, resource-intensive extraction procedures, and high water consumption. As the rate and scope of hardware updates rise in line with AI-driven needs, these adverse environmental impacts will most likely get worse, underscoring the need for sustainable practices during the device's lifetime.

The environmental problems brought on by artificial intelligence's explosive growth need thorough and aggressive answers. Adopting strategies including enhanced computation, sustainable operations, energy from renewable sources, and sustainable hardware, as well as software design, helps to substantially reduce the environmental consequences of artificial intelligence. This will ensure that future developments of artificial intelligence complement global climate targets.

Economic Costs of AI's Energy Footprint

In addition to changing technological environments, the rise of artificial intelligence is resulting in significant financial costs because of its high energy requirements. As artificial intelligence keeps expanding rapidly, the economic consequences of its computational needs become even more significant. These consequences influence the long-term investment plans of businesses, governmental entities, and educational institutions as well as their daily running expenses.

Growing Electricity Expenses in AI Activities

It takes a lot of processing power to run AI workloads, particularly training and inference jobs, which are often housed in data centers with high energy consumption. A significant amount of money is spent on power because of this necessity. Energy costs climb in tandem with the level of detail and complexity of AI models, especially huge models for languages like GPT-4 or complicated neural networks used for autonomous driving. The expenses associated with powering computing equipment can readily amount to millions of dollars annually in some organizations, rendering it a substantial element of operational expenditures.

To sustain their extensive AI infrastructure, digital giants such as Google, Amazon, Microsoft, and Meta consistently allocate billions of dollars each year. These expenses encompass the substantial electricity needed for cooling, as well as the power needed for compute clusters and GPUs. The substantial financial burden of handling the thermal consequences of AI workloads is shown by the fact that cooling may be responsible for up to 40% of the overall energy expenditures in AI-intensive data center operations.

Unexpected Expenses: Wear and Depreciation of Hardware

The financial effect of AI's environmental footprint extends beyond direct electricity prices and includes hardware expenditures as well. AI workloads are highly demanding, exerting significant pressure on CPUs, GPUs, TPUs, and Application-Specific Integrated Circuits or ASICs. This continuous, intensive usage significantly diminishes equipment lifespans by hastening device deterioration compared to conventional computing workloads. Increased capital expenditure and faster depreciation sometimes lead businesses to incur replacement costs, which substantially augment operating expenses. In contrast to conventional computing hardware, which can last up to five years under moderate workloads, GPUs utilized in AI training often require replacement after only two or three years of rigorous use. All these factors collectively increase the aggregate cost of management of AI facilities, hence imposing additional financial burdens on organizations.

Effects on Business Operations

AI's energy needs have an impact on operational strategy, resource allocation, and innovation potential in addition to directly affecting organizational expenses. Enterprises that heavily utilize AI are vulnerable to fluctuations in energy costs. AI-driven processes may be unexpectedly interrupted by fluctuating energy markets, thereby impacting overall strategy and company continuity. Such markets may be affected by disturbances resulting from climate change, the pace of renewable energy adoption, and geopolitical occurrences.

Market rivalry is also altered by this dynamic. While smaller enterprises often struggle to sustain AI-driven operations, larger companies with significant financial resources can absorb or alleviate increasing operational expenses. The expense associated with AI's energy demands intensifies pre-existing competitive inequalities and may reinforce market dominance for larger, affluent corporations to the detriment of incubation and smaller enterprises.

Case Study: Tech Giants' Investment Strategies

Leading technology businesses have made proactive investments in attempts to mitigate the economic impacts of energy-overloaded AI workloads. This proactive approach is demonstrated by Google, Meta, and OpenAI, which have made significant investments in hardware creativity, network optimization, and energy efficiency enhancements.

Additionally, OpenAI has made energy efficiency a top focus, especially as the level of detail and resource requirements of the latest models, such as GPT-4, continue to rise. Investing in model optimization techniques like quantization, trimming, and knowledge purification shows how algorithmic developments can significantly lower the computational requirements of implementing AI models at scale, as well as the corresponding energy and financial expenses.

Major cloud providers like AWS, Microsoft Azure, and Google Cloud are also constantly reinventing infrastructure architecture and administration. The need to proactively manage AI's economic ramifications is becoming more widely acknowledged.

In search of cost-balancing efficiency organizations must increasingly use energy-efficient practices at all operational levels to lessen the growing economic effects of AI's energy footprint. Promising paths to major cost reduction include investments in cutting-edge hardware, such as energy-efficient ASICs and neuromorphic computers, as well as enhancements in middleware management of resources and software-level optimizations.

Cost-effective AI operations are facilitated by a combination of energy-conscious software frameworks, effective computing algorithms, and ecological data center methods. The computational power needed for interpretation and training is successfully reduced by strategies like federated learning, which lowers data transport costs, and modeling compression techniques like quantization and pruning. Organizations can greatly cut the financial burden arising from energy-intensive AI workloads by using these techniques.
Businesses can lessen their susceptibility to unstable energy markets and improve their control over energy expenses by coordinating AI operating strategy with the availability of sources of clean energy and strategically placing data centers. Even though they need an initial investment, these steps set up businesses for long-term success and guarantee that AI's advantages will continue to be available and profitable.

The Urgent Need for AI Solutions That Are Sustainable

AI has boomed in the last decade. This has facilitated progress across various domains, including virtual assistants, driverless vehicles, and intricate financial analysis. Nonetheless, as previously stated, the swift expansion of artificial intelligence has been accompanied by substantial increases in energy consumption and environmental repercussions. To tackle this pressing issue, a substantial transition to sustainable artificial intelligence is necessary; this strategy prioritizes environmental stewardship and energy efficiency while maintaining performance and innovation.

"Green AI": Prioritising Efficiency Over Scale in the Concept's Adoption

The mainstream narrative of the growth of artificial intelligence has often emphasized model magnitude, computational intensity, and raw efficiency. This story effectively correlates larger models with superior outcomes. Nonetheless, it is no longer feasible to continue with this paradigm. A significant counterargument emphasizing the equivalence of efficiency and precision is the notion of "green AI." The notion of green artificial intelligence promotes the creation and application of models that optimize energy use, adhere to financial limitations, and minimize environmental impact.

The notion that enhanced computer capacity will necessarily yield proportional benefits is contested by the idea of "green artificial intelligence." Instead, it emphasizes the utilization of substantially fewer computational resources to achieve superior or equivalent performance. Efficiency-oriented research promotes the creation of solutions that deliver comparable or superior performance while substantially lowering energy and computational costs.

Researchers are increasingly concentrating on "efficiency benchmarks," which serve as incentives for models based not just on their accuracy but also on their computational and power consumption metrics. Rather than merely pursuing marginal performance gains at significant computational expenses, the objective is to optimize and maximize the value derived per unit of electricity utilized. This contrasts with the conventional method of seeking efficiency improvements. This change towards efficiency-focused evaluation generates a variety of impacts, promoting the development of artificial intelligence systems that are more sustainable, equitable, and accessible.

Optimization Techniques for Models: Efficient Strategies for Enhancing Energy Conservation

Substantial advancements in sustainable artificial intelligence may be achievable with the implementation of algorithmic optimization and innovative software methodologies. A multitude of optimization methods have been developed, demonstrating the considerable potential to substantially decrease computational demands while maintaining model correctness and performance. Among these strategies, quantization, knowledge distillation, and model pruning are particularly significant.

Model Optimisation Techniques:

Quantization:

- Involves reducing the precision of numerical values in models, such as transitioning from floating-point to fixed-point representation.
- Reduces computational load and memory usage without significant loss of accuracy.

Knowledge Distillation:

- A method where knowledge from a complex, computationally intensive model (teacher) is transferred to a simpler, efficient model (student).
- Enables smaller models to achieve comparable performance, greatly reducing energy consumption.

Model Pruning:

- Intentionally removes redundant or insignificant connections within neural networks.
- Has demonstrated reductions in computational demand ranging from 50% to 90%.
- Substantially decreases energy usage by simplifying the computational complexity.

Efficient Data Utilisation Techniques:

- Energy conservation in AI can also be significantly improved by optimizing data usage through several effective methodologies:
- Data Pruning:
- Removes unnecessary or redundant data points from training datasets.

- Results in faster training times and lower energy consumption without sacrificing model quality.

Data Augmentation:

- Enhances existing data by creating synthetic variations, thus reducing the need to collect or process large amounts of new data.
- Improves model performance while conserving computational resources.

Transfer Learning:

- Reuses pre-trained models on new tasks, significantly decreasing the amount of data and computing power required for training.
- Enables rapid deployment with minimal energy investment.
- Collectively, these optimization and data efficiency strategies hold substantial promise for reducing energy demands and promoting sustainable AI advancements.

Pruning the Model: Model pruning entails the intentional elimination of superfluous or trivial connections in neural networks, resulting in a substantial decrease in computing overhead and model complexity, while maintaining performance integrity. Researchers have effectively reduced the computing demands of advanced models by fifty to ninety percent, leading to a substantial decrease in energy consumption.

Knowledge Distillation: A successful technique termed knowledge distillation entails a bigger, previously trained model instructing a somewhat smaller, more energy-efficient model. This method enables the transfer of information and performance capabilities from resource-intensive large models to more lightweight models suitable for deployment on devices with low resources, such as mobile phones or edge computing environments.

These optimization techniques demonstrate how intentional, algorithmic advancements can effectively reduce the energy demands of artificial intelligence. They also suggest that effectiveness should not be compromised to attain sustainability. Efficiency-oriented strategies enhance accessibility while concurrently reducing expenses and democratizing technology. This is achieved by facilitating the deployment of artificial intelligence on technology with reduced power consumption.

Renewable resource-powered artificial intelligence: aligning AI with sustainability objectives

Nonetheless, other problems must be addressed before the complete implementation of artificial intelligence powered by renewable resources can occur. Despite the myriad benefits that renewable energy provides to the environment, it remains intermittently available and is dispersed unevenly across different regions globally. Enterprises utilizing green energy for artificial intelligence tasks generally require geo-distributed computing, which involves transferring workloads to locations abundant in renewable energy resources. This is executed to optimize energy procurement and diminish carbon footprints.

Recent Advancements in Computer Hardware and Algorithms

The development of specialist hardware for artificial intelligence enables the creation of sustainable AI solutions. Conventional graphics processing units are effective; nevertheless, they consume substantial amounts of electricity. Conversely, novel hardware solutions tailored for artificial intelligence tasks, including Google's Tensor Processing Units and Application-Specific Integrated Circuits, provide superior computational efficiency. Moreover, in contrast to traditional computing systems, these specialized processors may perform artificial intelligence computations more efficiently, hence decreasing the energy-per-operation measure.

Google's Tensor Processing Units are more efficient than conventional graphics processing units. TPUs are essential for the long-term advancement of artificial intelligence due to their superior performance coupled with markedly reduced energy usage. This is achieved by employing silicon specifically designed for the computation of AI tensors. Similarly, application-specific integrated circuits, designed specifically for certain AI functions, provide superior efficiency compared to conventional integrated circuits. Application-specific integrated circuits significantly diminish the power consumption necessary for computation-intensive applications, including computer vision, speech recognition, and natural language processing.

Regulation and policy fulfill a role within the system.

The European Union underscores the need for ethically and sustainably responsible artificial intelligence through efforts like the Artificial Intelligence Act and the Green Deal. This is achieved by integrating energy conservation into its strategic and legislative frameworks. Global legislation, which exhibits many similarities, underscores the imperative for a holistic strategy that incorporates social and environmental obligations alongside technological advancement.

One of the Collaborative Joint Obligations

It is essential for diverse stakeholders, including technology companies, educational institutions, governments, non-governmental organizations, and end users, to collaborate in addressing the sustainability issues posed by artificial intelligence. Through effective collaboration and mutual responsibility, these organizations can achieve substantial progress in artificial intelligence methodologies and facilitate a more expedited deployment of these techniques.

The acceleration of sustainability activities can be attained by the adoption of open-source projects and cross-industry collaborations that facilitate common knowledge bases, open programming and hardware frameworks, and standardized energy efficiency metrics. For instance, initiatives like the MLPerf benchmark offer established methodologies for assessing the computing efficiency of artificial intelligence. This allows organizations to transparently assess their sustainability performance.

Customers and the general public are essential in supporting companies that prioritize the development of responsible and energy-efficient artificial intelligence, as well as promoting practices that foster sustainable technology. Enhancing public awareness may motivate firms to integrate their technology strategies with sustainability objectives, perhaps resulting in increased demand for environmentally friendly artificial intelligence products.

Maintaining innovation sustainably is a key potential for the future. Quantum computing technology and neuromorphic architectures, which emulate the highly energy-efficient analytical processes of human neural systems, are two emerging technologies poised to transform the execution of artificial intelligence computational tasks. Both systems offer substantial improvements in energy efficiency. By optimizing resource utilization and minimizing unnecessary data movement, these technologies significantly reduce the power consumption associated with AI workloads. Such improvements are crucial for making AI deployment practical at scale, enabling more sustainable operations, lowering operational costs, and facilitating deployment in resource-constrained environments, such as edge computing or mobile applications.

The aggregate power demands of artificial intelligence systems may become too challenging to regulate without a robust dedication to sustainability. This is due to the growing digital interconnectedness of companies and societies. End users, organizations, policymakers, and artificial intelligence developers must reach a consensus that sustainability is an essential consideration in the future development of AI.

Chapter 2: Hardware for Energy-Efficient AI

Energy Efficient Processors for AI Applications and Workloads

The explosion of artificial intelligence and machine learning applications has greatly increased computing needs, therefore taxing traditional computer systems to their capacity. The processors performing substantial numerical computations and data processing, which require significant energy consumption, define the core of this computational intensity. The energy consumption associated with traditional computing systems, which rely solely on CPUs for all computational tasks, has become a major concern given the exponential growth in the scale and complexity of AI workloads. Consequently, there has been a marked shift toward developing energy-efficient processors and specialized hardware specifically designed for artificial intelligence applications.

Contemporary AI systems must handle vast data streams and computational activities, from basic arithmetic calculations to intricate concurrent matrix multiplications, which form the foundation of neural networks. Computers, despite their agility, are not always the best energy-efficient solution for computing tasks that are related to artificial intelligence. Artificial intelligence processors that are geared to improving performance while conserving energy have been developed in order to address these inefficiencies.

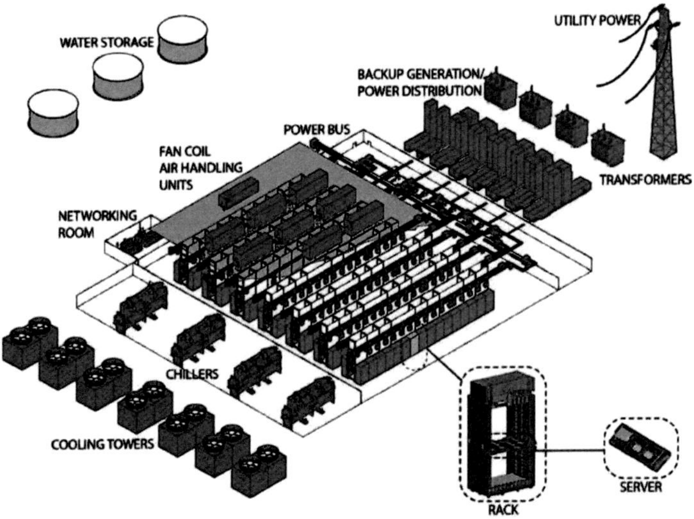

Source

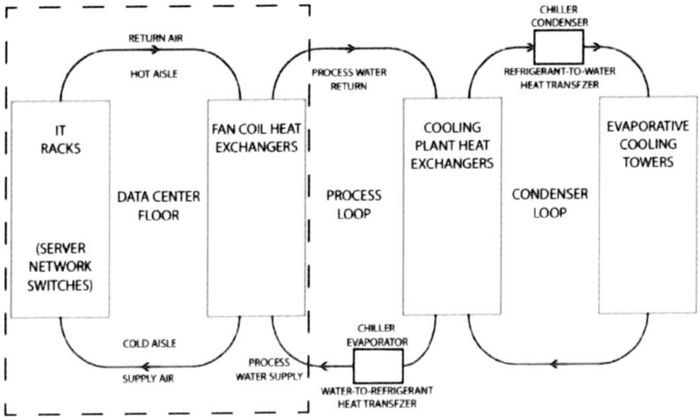

Source

Specialized AI processors (Google TPUs, NVIDIA GPUs, ARM processors, Intel Habana/Gaudi, FPGAs, Neuromorphic)

Google TPU: Specialized for matrix operations, very efficient (TPU v4)

An innovation is Google's TPU. TPUs represent specialised hardware specifically engineered for tensor computations essential for AI tasks, particularly neural networks. A TPU incorporates a design tailored towards matrix and vector processes, markedly decreasing energy consumption per computation. By focusing solely on AI computations, TPUs can eradicate the inefficiencies linked to general-purpose processors, hence significantly diminishing power utilization. The TPU v4 has enhanced energy efficiency relative to conventional CPUs and GPUs for analogous applications, attaining a huge improvement in performance-per-watt.

NVIDIA GPUs: Tensor cores optimized for AI workloads (H100, A100)

NVIDIA, a significant contender, has persistently advanced the limits of AI technology efficiency and effectiveness. Their most recent GPUs, such as the H100, utilise architectures with enhanced tensor cores created for deep learning tasks. These GPUs do highly parallel operations effectively, managing extensive matrix multiplications with negligible latency. Despite GPUs traditionally exhibiting more energy consumption than CPUs owing to their extensive parallelism, new design advancements have markedly greater efficiency per watt. Technologies include upgraded cooling systems, enhanced semiconductor processes, and optimised power management techniques, enabling these GPUs to sustain elevated computing performance while reducing overall power consumption.

ARM-based processors: Energy-efficient, used in mobile/edge devices

ARM processors have gained preference in energy-sensitive contexts, particularly in mobile and edge AI applications. ARM-based processors deliver energy-efficient computing via a reduced instruction set and optimised design, minimising energy usage while maintaining substantial computational capability. Apple and Qualcomm have effectively implemented ARM-based chips in mobile devices and peripheral AI devices, showcasing that these architectures may provide adequate performance for inference workloads while significantly reducing battery consumption relative to traditional CPU designs.

Intel's Gaudi and Habana: Efficient AI computations with Vector Neural Network Instructions

Intel has concentrated significantly on AI acceleration within its hardware. Intel's latest Gaudi and Habana AI accelerators are designed to deliver energy-efficient processing capabilities specifically for deep learning interpretation and learning. Intel's Xeon processors, equipped with sophisticated vector neural network instructions or in short VNNI, provide significant enhancements in AI-specific calculations. These processors effectively enhance AI tasks, optimising performance and energy consumption by minimising large data transfers between memory and processing units, a vital element in energy conservation.

FPGAs: Flexible, real-time reprogramming, energy-efficient for tailored applications

Field-programmable gate arrays, or FPGAs, have gained significance in AI acceleration. Firms like Xilinx (currently integrated with AMD) deliver FPGA-based solutions tailored for certain AI applications, presenting versatility and flexibility that conventional processors cannot rival. FPGAs enable developers to adapt computational pipelines for particular algorithms, facilitating highly optimised calculations specifically designed for AI workloads. The versatility of FPGAs allows for real-time reprogramming to accommodate diverse workloads, resulting in optimal resource utilisation and considerable energy conservation. FPGA accelerators are being effectively incorporated into data centres and edge devices, providing the necessary flexibility for specialised AI applications while maintaining energy economy.

Neuromorphic processors: Mimic biological neural systems, efficient event-driven computations

Neuromorphic processors, modelled after biological neural networks, exemplify a novel strategy for enhancing energy savings. Neuromorphic architectures, such as Intel's Loihi and IBM's TrueNorth, employ event-driven processing akin to the spiking mechanisms observed in organic neurons. In contrast to conventional processors that perpetually execute operations, neuromorphic processors engage only in reaction to events or inputs, significantly reducing energy usage for particular AI tasks. These computers emulate brain functions, providing remarkable efficiency for specific AI tasks like auditory processing, pattern identification, and decision-making in real time.

Recent advancements in hardware design encompass the incorporation of AI processing components within memory modules, referred to as processor-in-memory architectures. These devices seek to mitigate energy inefficiencies linked to data transfer throughout processors and memory elements, a significant energy expenditure in AI computations. PIM architectures drastically reduce energy usage over data transfers and enhance the speed of AI inference by integrating computing with data proximity.

Efficient processors are essential, however insufficient on their own. They must connect effortlessly with optimised software stacks, middleware, and advanced frameworks to fully achieve their potential. Hardware manufacturers are progressively providing tools and libraries that allow software to utilise processor capabilities efficiently, encompassing specialised programming sets and application-defined hardware administration for enhanced power efficiency. Nvidia's CUDA technology integrates physical features with software, enabling the efficient execution of intricate AI models while minimising resource wastage.

Experts in both academia and industry continually refine processor architectures to achieve improved energy efficiency and computational performance for artificial intelligence workloads. State-of-the-art semiconductor manufacturing processes, such as 5nm or smaller technology nodes, enable advancements like transistor miniaturization, better power gating, reduced leakage current, and sophisticated dynamic voltage and frequency scaling. These developments aim primarily at significantly lowering power consumption without compromising processing capabilities.

To gain deeper insights into selecting appropriate processor architectures for energy-efficient AI computing, it is essential to examine and compare the relative strengths, optimal use-cases, and limitations associated with each processor type:

Central Processing Units (CPUs) serve as versatile, general-purpose processors adept at handling diverse computing tasks. Their strong sequential processing capabilities and mature software ecosystems make CPUs ideal for workloads that involve complex control flow or require high flexibility. However, their general-purpose nature means they fall short in energy efficiency when executing massively parallel operations commonly found in AI model training and inference.

Graphics Processing Units (GPUs) excel at handling highly parallel tasks, such as those frequently encountered in deep learning computations. Their architecture, comprising thousands of parallel processing cores, is optimized for matrix and tensor operations. GPUs offer robust programming environments (e.g., NVIDIA's CUDA platform) that facilitate widespread adoption in training and inference tasks. However, while GPUs deliver outstanding parallel performance, they often consume more power than specialized hardware, making them less energy-efficient for fixed or repetitive AI workloads.

Tensor Processing Units (TPUs) and Application-Specific Integrated Circuits (ASICs) represent the highest tier of energy efficiency for specialized AI workloads. Designed explicitly for tensor computations, TPUs use systolic arrays for efficient matrix multiplication, significantly outperforming CPUs and GPUs in terms of power efficiency for dedicated tasks. ASICs like Google's

TPU are particularly suitable for stable, large-scale AI deployments in data centers. Despite their superior efficiency, ASICs lack flexibility, as they cannot adapt easily to algorithmic changes or diverse computing requirements.

Field-Programmable Gate Arrays (FPGAs) provide a unique balance between flexibility and efficiency. FPGAs can be dynamically reconfigured to handle varied computational tasks, making them ideal for adaptive AI applications, particularly in real-time environments or at the edge. While they offer lower power consumption compared to general-purpose GPUs, their programming complexity and moderate energy efficiency limit widespread adoption in fixed large-scale AI deployments.

Neuromorphic Processors offer revolutionary capabilities by emulating biological neural systems. Using spiking neural networks and event-driven processing, these processors achieve unparalleled energy efficiency in tasks involving real-time sensory data processing, robotics, and edge computing. Nevertheless, their specialized nature limits their applicability to broader, general-purpose AI workloads.

In conclusion, energy-efficient processors are essential in addressing the increasing energy requirements of contemporary AI workloads. TPUs, neuromorphic processors, optimised graphics processing unit designs, field-programmable gate arrays (FPGAs), and new developments in neuromorphic and memory-centric computing have all contributed to the significant advancement of hardware design in the direction of more energy-efficient computing paradigms.

Energy-Efficient Memory Architectures for AI

Conventional Memory Systems and Their Constraints

Memory systems have a major impact on AI applications' power efficiency because of how they manage performance and power consumption. Traditional memory technologies, such as DRAM and SRAM, have been cornerstones of computer systems for many years; nevertheless, they are encountering major efficiency challenges.

Dynamic Random-Access Memory is still one of the most commonly employed memory, for its considerable speed and density. Nonetheless, DRAM perpetually expends energy to update its storage cells, even during periods of inactivity, resulting in considerable power inefficiency. This continual refreshing amplifies inefficiencies, particularly in data-intensive AI tasks. SRAM (Static Random-Access Memory), characterised by superior data access rates compared to DRAM, exhibits more energy consumption per bit and reduced density, rendering it less suitable for huge-scale artificial intelligence applications that necessitate substantial capacity for memory.

These issues have prompted the investigation and application of advanced memory technologies designed for enhanced energy efficiency. The objective is to lower both static and dynamic power consumption, decrease the energy cost linked to frequent data transfers, and meet the extensive memory requirements of AI-driven operations.

Advanced memory technologies

Resistive Random Access Memory, Phase-Change Memory, Spin-Transfer Torque RAM, and Magnetoresistive Random Access Memory are all promising new non-volatile memory technologies that could solve the energy efficiency issues with traditional DRAM. These developments bring together the quick retrieval speed of volatile memory with the energy efficiency of non-volatility.

There has been a lot of buzz about phase-change memory due to its speed and longevity. By switching the memory cell's resistance between crystalline and amorphous states, PCM eliminates the requirement for constant power for information storage. In a similar vein, MRAM uses low-power, non-volatile magnetic tunnel couplings to store data, enabling quick performance.

These NVM systems offer significant energy reductions, especially in contexts characterised by frequent read-intensive processes typical of AI inference. They substantially reduced idle-state power consumption relative to DRAM, hence enhancing battery-operated and peripheral AI applications. As these technologies advance, their incorporation into memory structures can significantly diminish the energy consumption linked to AI data processing and storage.

- Dynamic Voltage and Frequency Scaling (DVFS): Dynamic Voltage and Frequency Scaling or DVFS is a technique employed to optimise power consumption in electronic devices. By adjusting the voltage and frequency according to the workload requirements, DVFS enhances energy efficiency while maintaining performance. This method is particularly beneficial in mobile and embedded systems, where battery life is paramount. The mechanism operates by monitoring the processor's workload and dynamically altering the operational parameters. When the demand is low, DVFS reduces the voltage and frequency, thereby decreasing power usage. Conversely, during high-demand scenarios, it increases these parameters to ensure adequate performance. Implementing DVFS requires sophisticated algorithms.

In practice, DVFS adjusts the voltage and frequency of operations in memory based on real-time workload monitoring, facilitating a balance amongst efficiency and energy consumption. For example, during extensive training or inference activities, AI models' memory components may function at elevated voltages and frequencies to achieve optimal performance. Conversely, during intervals of diminished computing activity, lowering voltage and frequency substantially conserves energy without markedly impairing performance.

Implementing DVFS in memory systems necessitates accurate feedback mechanisms to properly detect workload demands and dynamically modify memory parameters. This method significantly reduces energy consumption, particularly in situations when memory operations are infrequent or periodic, as commonly seen in practical AI applications. Thus, DVFS has emerged as a fundamental strategy in the construction of energy-efficient AI memory systems.

- Hybrid Memory Systems Incorporating Varied Storage Tiers: For maximum efficiency, hybrid memory systems use many storage layers, each with its own unique set of power characteristics, capacity, and performance. These devices provide the best of both worlds—optimal energy economy and the performance needed for AI applications—by cleverly combining different kinds of memory, such as DRAM, NVM, and traditional storage (like SSDs).

We can use stable technologies such as PCM or flash storage for data that is not accessed very frequently, and you can use faster, higher-power memory such as SRAM or DRAM for data which is accessed frequently but is not required. This hierarchical structure not only maximises power efficiency, but it also maximises speed and cost-effectiveness.

AI workloads, marked by varied and fluctuating data access patterns, greatly advantage from these tiered systems. Advanced management software may automatically optimise data placement and migration between tiers according to AI application requirements, hence enhancing productivity and overall system performance.

- Intelligent Memory Controllers for Enhanced Data Access: Intelligent memory controllers are essential for regulating data access patterns and greatly enhancing energy efficiency in AI applications. These controllers employ sophisticated algorithms and machine learning methods to predict, organise, and enhance memory access patterns, therefore minimising superfluous data transfers and decreasing energy consumption.

Traditionally, memory controllers adhere to predetermined, basic algorithms that lack the adaptability to respond dynamically to fluctuating AI workloads. Conversely, intelligent memory controllers utilise adaptive, predictive strategies that enhance memory operations by anticipating access trends, prefetching data, and implementing sophisticated scheduling methods to reduce idle times and information conflicts.

Memory controllers employing reinforcement learning can adjust to real-time fluctuations in AI workload behaviour, enhancing performance and power efficiency. These controllers dynamically forecast hot areas, proactively modify cache allocations, and efficiently handle transitions amongst active and inactive memory states.

Moreover, intelligent controllers frequently integrate temperature control and power gating techniques to reduce energy waste when segments of memory are inactive or underutilised. These strategies enhance overall energy-saving goals, rendering intelligent memory controllers essential in contemporary AI infrastructure.

Memory Caching and Intelligent Controllers

Memory caching is a crucial method for energy-efficient AI systems, since it reduces the overhead linked to constant and repetitive data transfers between processing units and main memory. Cache memory, typically utilising SRAM or specialised fast DRAM, briefly retains frequently accessible or recently utilised data, markedly enhancing access speeds and diminishing the energy expenditure linked to recurrently accessing slower, higher-capacity storage levels.

- Intelligent memory caching: Intelligent memory caching employs advanced techniques to anticipate what information must be cached, utilising complex heuristics and artificial intelligence algorithms. Predictive caching can markedly diminish delay and the energy expenditure linked to repetitive data retrievals. In AI applications like computer vision in real time or processing natural language, predictable data reuse behaviours can be effectively anticipated, reducing superfluous memory access and hence conserving energy.

The caching capabilities of intelligent controllers are improved through the dynamic modification of cache contents. Intelligent controllers make use of context-based demand evaluation in order to accomplish this goal. In multiprocessor artificial intelligence systems, data blocks are prioritised according to access regularity and job importance. Additionally, cache coherence is actively tested, and cache allocation sizes are dynamically changed. These controllers make a conscious decision regarding whether data should be stored, replaced, or removed from caches, which results in an improvement in both the efficiency of caches and the energy consumption associated with repetitive memory access.

Caching and intelligent memory managers provide a vital pair for energy-efficient memory architectures in artificial intelligence. They mitigate the performance constraints and energy losses associated with memory subsystem inefficiencies, providing optimised data flow and diminished energy consumption. These breakthroughs jointly guarantee scalable, efficient, and energy-conscious AI systems that meet contemporary computing requirements and sustainability objectives.

Contemporary intelligent memory processors are engineered to facilitate optimal data access for ever demanding AI workloads. As AI models increase in complexity and datasets expand, memory performance directly impacts system efficiency in general and responsiveness. Intelligent memory controllers tackle this issue by implementing dynamic optimisation algorithms to enhance data access patterns.

The principal function of smart controllers is to dynamically modify access priorities and schedule memory operations according to real-time workload analysis. Controllers employ AI-driven algorithms to recognise commonly requested datasets, effectively allocating data throughout memory channels to reduce access latency and use of energy. They execute data prefetching and optimise parallel access, substantially minimising idle periods and superfluous data transfers.

Furthermore, intelligent controllers incorporate power management techniques, like power gating, to disable inactive memory sections and minimise energy leakage. This fluid power management substantially decreases total energy usage, particularly during periods of low utilization. Moreover, controllers enhance data refresh intervals in volatile memory types, hence reducing superfluous energy use.

Data transport across several memory tiers is efficiently managed by intelligent controllers that interface with hybrid memory architectures. By transferring data that is accessed frequently to faster, more efficient memory and relegating data that is accessed seldom to more energy saving storage, these controllers significantly enhance memory performance and reduce overall power consumption.

They not only improve performance but also substantially diminish the energy consumption of memory operations, hence promoting the long-term viability and extensibility of AI systems.

Energy-Efficient Interconnections for Artificial Intelligence Systems

High-Speed Serializer-Deserializer for Efficient Data Transmission

Given that AI workloads necessitate elevated bandwidth and minimal latency, the efficacy of data transfer is becoming progressively vital. SerDes technology mitigates this difficulty by facilitating swift and effective data transfer among different parts of a system based on AI. SerDes chips transform parallel data streams into serial data streams to facilitate efficient transmission across high-speed communication paths, markedly diminishing the number of necessary communication lines and thereby lowering power consumption and signal interference.

- High-speed SerDes: This technology attains energy efficiency chiefly by reducing reliability of signal losses and enhancing throughput. By employing sophisticated modulation techniques like pulse amplitude modulation, SerDes systems attain elevated data rates within constrained bandwidth channels, significantly decreasing energy consumption per transmitted bit. Furthermore, contemporary SerDes utilize adaptive equalisation algorithms that dynamically rectify channel impairments, guaranteeing dependable, low-energy data transfer even at multi-terabit per second rates.

AI data centres predominantly depend on SerDes links embedded in processor interconnects as well as high-speed memory modules, markedly diminishing both latency and power demands for substantial data transfer. As AI systems expand, the use of rapid, power-efficient SerDes systems is essential to enhance performance without a corresponding rise in energy consumption, hence promoting more sustainable AI infrastructures.

Optical interconnects facilitate low-power, long-distance communication.

Regarding the ever-increasing energy efficiency concerns that AI infrastructures confront, optical interconnects have shown to be a game-changer. More sustainable and energy-conscious solutions are urgently needed due to the rising scale of modern AI systems, which include communication across chips, boards, servers, and even racks. As an effective substitute that may significantly reduce energy consumption in comparison to electrical interconnects, optical interconnects have emerged as a strong contender.

By directly combining optical and electrical components on a single semiconductor substrate, photonic technologies, especially silicon photonics, provide a revolutionary approach. Silicon photonics is a method of creating small, efficient modules that integrate photonic components like waveguides, modulators, and photodetectors with traditional electronic circuits. Signal transmission over short to medium distances inside data centres or HPC systems is made much simpler and uses much less energy as a result of this integration.

The ability to maintain very fast data transfer speeds with very little power per bit is the fundamental benefit of silicon photonics. By taking advantage of established methods for fabricating semiconductors, silicon photonics technology enables the mass production of optical components that are integral to silicon chips at a reasonable cost. Thus, silicon photonics interconnects can currently sustain data transmission rates in the multi-terabit-per-second range, which is significantly more efficient and has substantially greater bandwidth than conventional copper-based alternatives. In comparison to conventional electrical interconnects, these innovations not only speed up data transmission but also significantly reduce power overhead, cutting energy consumption per transferred bit by many orders of magnitude.

Optical connectivity technology can significantly reduce cooling needs, operational expenses, and power consumption in AI-driven infrastructures. Cooling expenses account for a significant amount of data centre energy expenditures; optical links naturally produce far less heat than electrical ones, which directly correlates to decreased cooling costs. Additional monetary and ecological benefits result from longer component life and reduced power usage per data transaction made possible by better thermal control.

Not only do optical interconnects reduce power consumption right away, but they also make systems far more flexible and scalable. Optical technologies always keep a high level of efficiency, unlike electrical alternatives that inevitably experience diminishing returns as system complexity and transmission lengths increase. Optical interconnects are ideal for future exascale computing environments and large-scale distributed AI systems due to their scalability. Optical connectivity technology allows for cost-effective and flexible scaling solutions in AI data centres and cloud infrastructures, unlike electrical linkages, which experience exponential power consumption increases.

In addition, unlike copper-based interconnects, optical technologies greatly improve signal integrity and do away with electromagnetic interference. Data centres with a high concentration of electronic interference might have performance degradation, necessitating energy-intensive shielding and signal regeneration. However, optical signalling does not suffer from electromagnetic interference or crosstalk, so it can transmit signals reliably and accurately over greater distances without the need for extra power-hungry signal regeneration processes. Because of this, energy efficiency is further improved through the use of simpler system designs with fewer active components.

There is a dramatic decrease in the energy overhead associated with transmission integrity and cooling requirements when using optical communication lines because of the low levels of electromagnetic wave interference, signal attenuation, and heat generation. This technology allows for expandable, energy-efficient long-distance connectivity.

Network-on-Chip (NoC): Reduce latency and energy on-chip

Network on Chip architectures are designed to minimise latency in integrated circuits. By employing a structured interconnection framework, these architectures facilitate efficient communication between various components of a system-on-chip. The primary objective is to enhance data transfer speeds while reducing the time taken for signal propagation. NoC architectures utilize many communication paths, enabling parallel data transmission and so alleviating bottlenecks associated.

Network-on-Chip designs have become vital solutions to mitigate the increasing energy consumption issues in AI devices. In contrast to conventional bus-based interconnects, NoC offers a scalable, flexible, and energy-efficient method for enabling communication among several on-chip components. Integrating a network with packet switching directly onto the silicon die greatly decreases latency and energy usage relative to traditional connecting methods.

Using complex algorithms for routing and resource allocation schemes, NoC systems optimise data transport at the chip level, resulting in efficiency. The limitations of traditional bus designs, such as signal delay, contention, and high power consumption, are eliminated by Network-on-Chip, allowing for fast and scalable communication across various functional components such as memory modules, accelerators, and CPU cores. Optimising data transmission based on flow patterns and workload parameters, adaptive routing algorithms are used in advanced Network-on-Chip architectures. This improves energy efficiency by reducing congestion and unnecessary data hops.

The capacity of NoCs to flexibly regulate data flows efficiently renders them especially beneficial for AI workloads, characterised by heavy and concurrent processing requirements. Thus, NoC architectures markedly reduce the total energy consumption, enhance system responsiveness, and offer essential assistance for the development of energy-efficient AI hardware systems.

Wireless Interconnects for Adaptable and Expandable Systems

Wireless connectivity solutions are becoming increasingly appealing for AI systems that demand flexibility, scalability, and low power consumption, particularly in extensive and distributed configurations. Wireless interconnects eliminate physical cabling limitations, facilitating reconfigurable, modular architectures that can be easily scaled or rearranged to meet diverse AI application requirements.

Energy-Conscious Routing Algorithms for Enhanced Data Transmission

Optimising data flows in AI systems is crucial for energy-aware routing algorithms, which have a direct impact on energy use and performance efficiency. Algorithms like these reduce energy usage per transmitted bit by reducing the number of intermediate hops and congestion-induced delays caused by data packet routing strategy along optimal paths. They efficiently distribute load across several pathways, hence minimizing hotspots and power-demanding nodes within network systems.

Advanced routing algorithms utilise machine learning and heuristic methods to anticipate traffic trends and proactively optimise routes. In extensive AI implementations, particularly in data centres or distant AI systems, these sorts of algorithms markedly reduce energy consumption associated with superfluous data transfers and extraneous computations. Moreover, these solutions provide dynamic adaptability to fluctuating workloads, guaranteeing that routing decisions consistently coincide with energy efficiency objectives.

Hardware Accelerators for Energy-Efficient Artificial Intelligence

Application-Specific Integrated Circuits for Specialised AI Functions

Application-Specific Integrated Circuits have become a preeminent solution for tackling the energy issues from the rapid expansion of artificial intelligence. In contrast to general processors, ASICs are specifically designed for particular AI functions, including neural network inference and training. This focused design markedly eliminates superfluous computing burden, resulting in substantial increases in power economy and computational throughput.

The ASIC design specificity enables such chips to eliminate unnecessary instructions and hardware components present in general-purpose processors, thus reducing power consumption per operation by a great margin. ASICs utilize optimized transistor configurations and reduced architectures to efficiently handle recurrent, highly parallelizable operations common in deep learning systems. Such examples include Google's Tensor Processing Units, designed specifically to improve tensor computations crucial for machine learning models. TPU structures offer significantly better performance-per-watt than the conventional CPUs or GPUs through incorporation of specialized matrix multiplication processors and optimized data pathways.

However, the specialization of ASICs involves some compromises. While they have unmatched energy frugality and performance for dedicated tasks, their rigidity could limit their scope. ASICs are not as easily reprogrammable or flexible for fresh or varied tasks, necessitating additional investments when algorithms change radically. In steady and well-understood circumstances, ASICs deliver unparalleled power efficiency and performance, enabling sustainable scaling of complex AI models and reducing operating costs and environmental consequences of power consumption by orders of magnitude.

Field-Programmable Gate Arrays are platforms for reconfigurable acceleration.

Field-Programmable Gate Arrays are powerful hardware accelerators more widely used in artificial intelligence because they have a unique combination of flexibility and energy efficiency. In opposition to ASICs, whose state is permanent after manufacturing, FPGAs bring the runtime reprogramming possibility to the table, allowing AI programmers to re-tune hardware acceleration dynamically as per evolving AI algorithms and workload needs. Reconfigurability by FPGAs is profoundly helpful for AI infrastructure characterized by rapidly evolving algorithms or varying job mixes, as this allows immediate hardware changes in the field without design changes being needed.

FPGAs achieve energy efficiency by providing parallelism that is customized for specific algorithms, thus reducing unnecessary computations. Neural network algorithms require high amounts of parallel computation that can easily be distributed into FPGA systems. FPGA accelerators, such as those provided by AMD, perform better in cases requiring customizability and flexiblility in computing, including edge AI, real-time inference, and rapid prototyping of AI models. The programmable nature of FPGAs is beneficial for low-latency inference workloads.

FPGAs offer a flexible middle ground between general-purpose CPUs and tailored ASICs, offering better efficiency compared to CPUs and greater flexibility than ASICs. With advancements in AI models and techniques, FPGA-based accelerators can adapt quickly, with ongoing improvements.

Graphics Processing Units with Optimised Tensor Cores

With their parallel processing power, GPUs have totally revolutionized the computer world when it comes to AI, with deep learning computations becoming a piece of cake. GPU architecture, particularly from Nvidia and AMD, feature Tensor Cores—dedicated processors—designed to accelerate tensor and matrix computation, something ubiquitous in AI models. With Tensor Cores, compute operations such as convolutions, matrix multiplications, and vector figures run much faster using much lower power consumption.

Nvidia's GPU architecture, such as the Ampere-based A100, the latest H100 family and the upcoming Blackwell chips, demonstrates power-efficient designs specifically for AI workloads. Tensor Cores in those GPUs offer mixed-precision arithmetic, including FP16 (half-precision), FP32 (single-precision), and INT8 (integer operations), thus supporting flexible and power-efficient computations. Mixed-precision arithmetic significantly reduces energy consumption per operation by allowing lower-precision computation without compromising significantly on accuracy. The use of FP16 arithmetic saves power by half compared to FP32 for certain inference workloads, leading to large energy savings in data centers and edge computing environments.

GPUs feature effective memory layouts and sophisticated power management techniques to optimize data transportation costs. New-generation features, such as CUDA-based software stacks, improve energy efficiency by optimising software and hardware resources more effectively, reducing idle times, and boosting utilisation.

Neuromorphic processors enable brain-inspired computation.

Neuromorphic computers represent a breakthrough approach to AI computing by simulating natural neural networks in silicon hardware. Biological neural architectures-inspiring neuromorphic processors use spiking neural networks for event-based computation, turning on only in response to input events, similar to biological neurones. Event-based structure significantly reduces energy consumption by eliminating unnecessary computations, making neuromorphic processors very energy-efficient for specific AI applications.

Intel's Loihi and IBM's TrueNorth demonstrate modern advances in neuromorphic technology, with impressive gains in efficiency for sensory processing, object recognition, and real-time pattern matching. Neuromorphic computers mimic biological brain functioning and employ sparse connectivity to provide low-power solutions well-suited for edge devices, IoT sensors, robotics, and a number of other applications that require efficient real-time decision-making ability.

While neuromorphic processors provide energy benefits, they are specialized and lack the general programmability of conventional architectures at present. With advancing technology, neuromorphic hardware is expected to become more and more crucial for the sustainable and energy-efficient deployment of AI.

Systolic arrays enable effective matrix multiplication through a parallel processing architecture. The structure consists of a network of interconnected processing elements that compute and pass data rhythmically. Each element conducts an individual operation on the input matrices, which enables calculations simultaneously while reducing latency. Systolic array designs aim to optimise data movement in a manner such that the appropriate inputs for processing units become available at appropriate moments, thereby providing improved throughput. The arrangements in these arrays are adaptable to -

- Systolic arrays are specialized hardware accelerators designed to support precise and high-throughput operations of matrix multiplications, a critical computation in artificial intelligence processing, particularly in deep neural network computations.
- Systolic arrays consist of connected processing units structured in a grid pattern to support continuous, rhythmic, and concurrent data flow similar to synchronized contraction of the heartbeat, thus the name "systolic."

Systolic systems achieve significant power efficiency and performance gains through data streamlining and localised processing stimulation. Within a systolic cluster, every computation element only communicates with its immediate neighbours, thus eliminating the need for complex and power-hungry long-range data exchanges. This localised arrangement dramatically reduces total latency as well as electrical usage compared to conventional parallel architectures.

A great example of systolic arrays can be found in Google's Tensor Processing Units that extensively use this architecture for deep learning computations. TPUs leverage systolic arrays to efficiently conduct matrix multiplication computations that are integral to neural network operations. Systolic arrays improve energy efficiency by providing an enhanced computation pathway and lessening data communication, thereby allowing sustainable and economical execution of big-scale neural networks.

ASICs, FPGAs, GPUs with optimized tensor cores, neuromorphic processing units, and systolic arrays are all part of a powerful suite of hardware accelerators. Each of these accelerators has its own advantages in terms of making energy efficiency of AI workloads better, overall enabling sustainable and scalable AI development across numerous applications and use cases.

Neuromorphic Computing for Energy-Efficient Artificial Intelligence

Spiking Neural Networks for Event-Driven Computation

Neuromorphic computing represents a tremendous departure from traditional computing methods, which are directly inspired by biological neural networks. Unlike traditional neural networks that use continuous numerical values and perform extensive computations at every timestep, spiking neural networks (SNNs) make use of discrete spikes or events for data transmission and hence significantly reduce energy consumption by preventing redundant computation.

The event-driven nature of SNNs allows the systems to spend most of their time in a quiescent state, drawing little energy until a relevant input event triggers brain activity. On triggering, the devices rapidly transfer signals across an interconnected network of neuron-like nodes that communicate with each other by synchronized electrical signals, very similar to the operations of biological synapses. The technique minimizes unnecessary power use quite substantially, making SNNs ideal for use in scenarios that require uninterrupted, real-time sensing and processing under tight energy constraints.

Well-known implementations of neuromorphic hardware based on spiking neural networks are Intel's Loihi chip, with millions of artificial neurones for low-power spike-based computing, and IBM's TrueNorth processor, which employs tightly coupled neurosynaptic cores to realize significant power savings over conventional computing implementations in real-time sensory processing applications. Employing neuromorphic designs enables the creation of advanced AI solutions that exactly mimic cognitive processes without compromising ultra-low power consumption necessary for actual applications.

Emerging Non-Volatile Memory: Memristors for Synaptic Adaptability

Memristors are becoming ubiquitous components in neuromorphic devices, offering unique functionalities well-suited for brain-inspired computing. A memristor is an electronic device of two terminals that has resistance controllable in an adaptive way according to the previous history of electric impulses passed through it. It closely resembles how biological synaptic plasticity works in human brains through the modification of synapse strength as the vital way of brain adaptation and learning.

The intrinsic ability of memristors to mimic synaptic functionality is the basis of neuromorphic realization of plasticity in the brain. Plasticity, or the adaptive modulation of neuronal connections, is fundamental to memory and learning development in biological brains. Mimicking this functionality with classical silicon technology is energy-expensive and inefficient. Memristors, on the other hand, can perform synaptic functions directly, allowing localised computation and drastically reducing the energy cost associated with synaptic updates.

In addition, memristors can be very compactly built into crossbar arrays, which is especially suited for neuromorphic applications. These arrays permit very high-parallel computation, performing the multiplication and addition operations that form the basis for brain calculations straight away in the memory without switching data between computational and storage systems. Experimental neuromorphic chips using memristive devices promise outstanding computational densities, low latencies, and great energy efficiencies, making them well-suited for edge and embedded artificial intelligence applications that demand cognitive-like levels of processing expertise.

Neuromorphic Architectures for Cognitive Computing

Brain-inspired architectures represent a dramatic departure from traditional von Neumann computer designs, emulating directly the structure and operational rules that underlie biological neural networks. The human brain, an incredibly efficient computing machine, accomplishes complex mental functions with a relatively modest energy expenditure. Neuromorphic hardware designs seek to mimic the neuronal and synaptic activity in biological networks for comparable efficiency.

These brain-inspired architectures have large parallel arrays of neuron-like computing elements connected by adaptive synapses, mimicking the distributed, parallel processing of biological brains. Unlike conventional computing paradigms, brain-inspired architectures focus on dispersed computation, sparse activity, and adaptive learning processes, leading to significantly lower energy usage.

Brain inspired computer architectures tend to support event-driven, asynchronous evaluation models that reduce energy usage by processing data only when relevant changes occur. This asynchronous approach enhances scalability and fault tolerance, making these systems particularly well-suited for complex cognitive computing tasks.

Brain inspired hardware is increasingly significant, with applications proliferating in robotics, edge computing, and intelligent sensor networks. As these architectures advance, they provide substantial energy efficiency improvements for various next-generation cognitive AI applications.

Utilisation of Neuromorphic Computing in Robotics and Sensing

Neuromorphic computing has shown significant advantages in energy economy for robotics and sensor computing applications. Robotics and sensory systems frequently necessitate real-time processing of continuous sensor data, pattern identification, and swift decision-making. Conventional computing paradigms have difficulties in executing these jobs successfully because of the persistent high-power data processing requirements.

Neuromorphic hardware, utilising event-driven and brain-inspired architectures, effectively manages these streaming data workloads. Robotic systems employing neuromorphic processors, such as Intel's Loihi, can swiftly interpret sensory signals, process them sequentially, and promptly initiate suitable actions such as evasion of obstacles, localisation, and navigation—without the energy burden linked to constant computation. This real-time, event-driven methodology markedly enhances battery longevity and operational efficacy, rendering neuromorphic technology exceptionally beneficial for independent mobile robots and drones functioning in energy-limited settings.

In sensor networks, neuromorphic computers adeptly analyse chaotic and sparse inputs from sensory systems, such as auditory or visual signals, by handling spikes that correlate to significant changes rather than whole data streams. These processors are highly effective in embedded AI systems, security cameras, and environmental monitoring devices, significantly diminishing energy consumption for data processing. Neuromorphic systems, by mimicking biological sensory processing, provide significant enhancements in efficiency of energy, latency, and robustness for real-time detection and autonomous applications in robotics.

Obstacles and Prospective Trajectories of Neuromorphic Hardware

Despite the considerable potential exhibited by neuromorphic computing, some major problems persist that must be resolved to guarantee its extensive acceptance and efficacy.

Initially, programming and software tools remain in their infancy within the neuromorphic field. In contrast to conventional CPU and GPU architectures, neuromorphic systems do not possess established, standardised software stacks, frameworks, and development environments, hence hindering their adoption. Creating efficient programming frameworks, intuitive software interfaces, and accessible developer communities is crucial for promoting widespread adoption across various industries.

Secondly, creating neuromorphic technology that reliably attains high precision and adaptability across many activities is difficult. Neuromorphic processors presently excel in specialised, event-driven functions such as perception of sensation and pattern recognition. Nonetheless, they encounter difficulties in generalising over more extensive, less-structured AI tasks usually managed by deep learning systems. Future research should concentrate on improving the adaptability and applicability of neuromorphic networks to more efficiently tackle intricate cognitive computing challenges.

Furthermore, the production and dependability of neuromorphic hardware, particularly components like memristors, remain substantial technical challenges. Memristive technologies demonstrate fluctuation in device attributes, constrained endurance, and possible deterioration over time. Issues of reliability and uniformity might affect the consistency of overall performance and the dependability of the system, hence constraining practical applications. Enhancing the manufacturing accuracy, stability, and durability of memristor-based components is essential for realizing the complete potential of neuromorphic hardware.

A key domain for future investigation is to the scalability of neuromorphic systems to accommodate greater and more intricate workloads. Current prototypes exhibit success at constrained scales; nevertheless, realising effective large-scale implementations necessitates addressing connectivity complexities, heat management challenges, and the efficient integration of varied computational components on a unified platform.

Ultimately, promoting standardisation within the neuromorphic ecosystem is essential. Establishing standards for hardware connections, programming models, and efficiency benchmarks will expedite acceptance and integration with traditional computer environments. The establishment of specialised, open-source development platforms and comprehensive libraries is essential to empower a broader community of academics and developers to contribute to and improve neuromorphic systems.

Confronting these difficulties by ongoing research, partnerships among academia and industry, especially advances in neuromorphic computing technology, can yield significant improvements in energy efficiency. Neuromorphic technologies, incorporated into comprehensive AI ecosystems, provide promising avenues for developing viable, scalable cognitive computing designs necessary to address the growing needs of intelligent machines in an energy-limited environment.

Hardware Accelerators for Energy-Efficient AI Application-Specific Integrated Circuits (ASICs) for Dedicated AI Tasks Revisited Application-Specific Integrated Circuits (ASICs) continue to be essential for the attainment of exceptional energy efficiency and performance in dedicated AI applications. These specialised hardware accelerators are meticulously optimised for specific algorithms, such as neural network inference, resulting in significant power and performance enhancements in comparison to general-purpose hardware. ASICs accomplish this efficiency by eliminating unnecessary instruction overhead and providing circuitry that is specifically optimised for tasks such as convolutional neural network analysing, recurrent neural networks, or transformer-based frameworks.

An ASIC that is specifically designed to accelerate machine learning operations is Google's TPU. This is a notable example. The computational efficiency of TPUs is considerably improved while power consumption is minimised, as they employ systolic array architectures for matrix multiplication. In the same vein, Tesla's Full Self-Driving or FSD chip, a custom ASIC that is specifically designed for real-time inference activities in autonomous vehicles, significantly reduces energy consumption and latency in comparison to general-purpose alternatives. Nevertheless, ASICs are inherently inflexible once they are fabricated, which restricts their adaptability to algorithmic evolution. Nevertheless, ASICs are indispensable components of contemporary AI hardware strategies, providing unparalleled energy efficiency, cost savings, and performance in stable or highly repetitive AI tasks.

Quantum Computing for AI with Low Energy Consumption

For certain artificial intelligence jobs, quantum computing is a new paradigm that has the potential to significantly increase computational speed and energy efficiency. In contrast to conventional computing, which uses bits that are either 0 or 1, quantum computing makes use of quantum bits, or qubits, that can exist in several states at once. For some particular situations, quantum processors may execute complicated parallel calculations significantly more effectively than their classical equivalents thanks to this fundamental characteristic, known as superposition, and quantum entanglement.

The special benefit that quantum computing provides in terms of computational speed and energy economy is demonstrated by quantum algorithms, such as Grover's search algorithm, Shor's factoring algorithm, and quantum-inspired optimization algorithms. Quantum algorithms have the potential to greatly speed up machine learning model training, optimize intricate neural networks, and effectively tackle optimization issues that are computationally and energy-intensive on traditional hardware.

However, there are still many technological obstacles to overcome before quantum computing can be widely used, including preserving qubit coherence, error correction, and the scalability of quantum hardware. Notwithstanding these drawbacks, quantum computing's incorporation into the AI computer ecosystem, akin to neuromorphic computing, offers a viable path toward the realization of sustainable and energy-efficient computing in next AI applications.

Comparative Analysis and Use Cases of GPUs and TPUs

Graphics Processing Units and Tensor Processing Units are two prominent categories of hardware accelerators that are extensively employed in contemporary AI systems. Each class has its own unique advantages and specific applications.

Thousands of parallel cores are utilised by GPUs, which are ideal for broad-application parallel workloads, and have been popularised by companies such as NVIDIA and AMD. This enables them to execute multiple computations simultaneously. GPUs have historically been the dominant technology for AI training due to their robust software ecosystems, programmability, and flexibility (e.g., CUDA by Nvidia). Specialised hardware components that are optimised for multiplication by matrix, convergence, and tensor operations are utilised by modern GPUs, particularly those that are endowed with tensor cores such as the Nvidia H100 or A100, to efficiently execute deep learning tasks. GPUs' adaptability enables them to manage a wide range of workloads, including real-time inference activities in fields such as autonomous vehicles, processing pictures, and sophisticated scientific simulations, as well as the training of vast deep learning models.

Conversely, TPUs are ASICs that are specifically designed to accelerate machine learning workloads and are purpose-built. TPUs, which were created by Google, are designed to optimise tensor computations at a high throughput while minimising power consumption per operation. TPUs are particularly effective in large-scale training scenarios and deep learning inference, as they offer superior energy savings and throughput compared to GPUs for matrix-heavy calculation as a result of their designated systolic array architecture. This advantage is plainly demonstrated by the seamless integration of Google's TPU platform with TensorFlow: it significantly accelerates inference workloads at lower energy costs compared to GPUs.

The primary criteria for selecting between GPUs and TPUs for a particular use case are application-specific computational demands, power requirements, and flexibility. GPUs are the preferred choice for algorithmic developments that necessitate versatility, clinical AI research, or heterogeneous workloads. Conversely, TPUs offer the most efficient energy consumption and optimal performance for frequent deep learning inference operations in data centres or stable, large-scale production environments. Consequently, the strategic decision between GPUs and TPUs is contingent upon how particular computational complexity of AI tasks, the flexibility demands, and the characteristics of the burden.

Power Losses in Electrical Power Chains and Power Delivery

Energy efficiency in AI data centres is heavily reliant on power supply infrastructure in addition to computer hardware. Energy losses are naturally introduced by components including transformers, power distribution units, cables, and connectors through electrical resistance and voltage conversion. Uninterruptible power supply and voltage regulators alone can cause efficiency losses of 5–15%, while cables and connectors contribute minor but cumulative losses.

Advanced solutions including digital power management, direct-current power distribution designs, and high-efficiency voltage regulators must be implemented in order to reduce these losses. Data centres can greatly improve their overall energy efficiency and sustainability by reducing conversion stages and utilizing effective infrastructure.

Key Innovations in Energy-Efficient Hardware: A Summary

The landscape of energy-efficient AI hardware has been significantly influenced by a number of important innovations, which have allowed for the deployment of more complex AI models while simultaneously reducing power consumption.

- Initially, specialised ASICs, particularly Google's TPU, have established new benchmarks for energy efficiency in devoted AI computations, substantially surpassing general-purpose hardware. ASICs significantly decrease the need for electricity for specific, repetitive duties by eliminating unnecessary computational overhead.

- Secondly, GPUs that are endowed with optimised tensor cores exhibit advanced AI training, which is achieved by utilising mixed-precision arithmetic (FP16, INT8) to significantly reduce energy consumption without sacrificing significant performance. This optimisation, in conjunction with enhanced semiconductor manufacturing processes, establishes GPUs as energy-efficient and adaptable accelerators.

- Furthermore, Field-Programmable Gate Arrays provide a distinctive combination of adaptability and energy efficiency that is essential for real-time or evolving AI applications. Their reconfigurability is essential for dynamic applications, as it offers a compromise between GPU flexibility and ASIC efficiency.

Neuromorphic computing has introduced altogether new paradigms of energy savings by directly emulating biological processes in hardware, utilising brain-inspired spiking neural networks and memristors. Optical interconnects, Network-on-Chip, and rapid connectivity SerDes are among the emerging interconnect solutions that have enhanced data transmission efficacy, thereby reducing system-wide power overhead.

These innovations collectively demonstrate the ongoing convergence of advanced semiconductor technologies, cognitive power management tactics, and hardware specialisation, thereby establishing the groundwork for energy-efficient, sustainable AI implementations in a variety of use cases.

Chapter 3: Middleware for Energy-Efficient AI

AI-Powered Energy-Efficient Resource Management

An essential component in the development of scalable and sustainable AI systems is energy-efficient resource management. The fundamental system must constantly adjust to satisfy performance needs without consuming needless power as AI workloads increase in complexity and size. This calls for a middleware layer that can allow lightweight activities on edge devices, control temperature profiles, integrate virtual machines, and distribute resources wisely. The objective is to maximize productivity whilst reducing financial and environmental expenses by finding a balance between computing effectiveness and power economy.

Allocating Resources Dynamically Depending on Workload Demands

Dynamic resource allocation is the foundation of AI middleware that is energy-aware. Dynamic allocation of resources adjusts computation, memory, and data to the workload's current needs in real-time, as opposed to static resource supplies, which allocate a fixed number of resources irrespective of consumption. Tasks involving AI training and inference frequently vary in intensity, needing minimum resources at certain points and GPU power bursts at others. By having the ability to scale capabilities up or down, middleware with load tracking and prediction features helps prevent energy waste from over-provisioned or idle parts.

An AI model training pipeline, for example, might use several GPUs for forward and backward passes, but just a small portion of that might be required for data preparation or model evaluation. Middleware platforms such as resource schedulers and Kubernetes can monitor CPU/GPU use, memory bandwidth, and temperature profiles and modify allocations via dynamic scaling. This increases system efficiency by saving energy and freeing up assets for other uses.

Power-Conscious VM Integration

AI workloads are still frequently run in virtual machines, particularly in cloud and hybrid systems. On the other hand, unused hosts or idle virtual machines can greatly increase power usage. By combining low-utilization virtual machines with reduced physical machines, a technique known as power-aware virtual machine convergence enables idle hosts to be shut down or put into low-power modes.

This method depends on sophisticated orchestration systems that can assess resource usage trends and make migration choices at the moment. For instance, an amalgamation engine can live-migrate virtual machines onto a single server while shutting down the others if they are all utilizing less than 30% of the CPU and memory on different physical hosts. Live migration offers significant energy savings with little interruption to ongoing operations.

Workload affinity rules, which prevent resource-heavy or thermally susceptible virtual machines from being grouped together, and QoS-aware policies, which maintain optimal performance while maximizing power consumption, are examples of further improvements. VM consolidation provides a strong basis for flexible, energy-efficient infrastructure when paired with dynamic allotment.

Energy-Proportional Calculation

Energy-proportional computing, which holds that power consumption should increase linearly with task intensity, is one of the fundamental ideas of contemporary server design. Unfortunately, even when overused, a lot of traditional systems use a lot of baseline power, which results in inefficiencies. Because it may selectively disable unwanted components and modulate resource utilization, middleware is essential to ensuring proportionality.

Advanced power states, such as AMD's Cool'n'Quiet or Intel's SpeedStep, for example, enable middleware to reduce CPU voltage and frequency when there is less load. It is also possible to deactivate memory banks, park unused GPUs, and pause I/O controllers. The middleware layer's software-defined energy guidelines can instantly modify system settings to guarantee that energy consumption closely matches workload needs.

Advanced power states such as AMD's Cool'n'Quiet, Intel's SpeedStep, and regular processor power states like P-states and C-states allow middleware to dynamically change CPU voltage and frequency depending on workload needs. Apart from CPUs, middleware can control energy efficiency via turning off memory banks, parking underutilised GPUs, and I/O controller pauses. When efficiently used by middleware, hardware-level characteristics such clock gating and power gating greatly lower idle power use between tasks. By means of software-defined energy policies, the middleware layer can quickly change system settings to match energy use with real-time performance requirements.

In large-scale data centres, for instance, systems like Microsoft Azure and Google Cloud use dynamic resource scheduling and power-aware orchestration to aggregate workloads during off-peak hours, therefore allowing idle servers to enter low-power modes. Likewise, mobile SoCs use DVFS and aggressive power gating to prolong battery life without affecting user experience.

AI infrastructure can achieve significantly improved overall energy efficiency by aiming for energy proportionality, especially in shared environments where numerous processes run concurrently and unpredictably.

Resource Management with Thermal Awareness

Energy efficiency includes controlling heat in addition to electricity use. Data centres and edge devices with thermal hotspots may experience performance degradation, hardware ageing, and the need for active cooling, all of which raise power consumption. By proactively allocating tasks to preserve thermal balance, thermally aware resource management allays these worries.

Thermal-aware throttling has a significant positive impact on on-device AI systems, like those found in smartphones and drones. These systems can prolong battery life and avoid thermal shutdowns by limiting processing intensity, lowering frame rates, or switching to lower-power models in response to growing temperature profiles.

Resource Management for Edge AI

There are particular energy issues associated with the spread of AI to the edge, such as on embedded systems, mobile CPUs, and IoT devices. Optimizing constrained compute, memory, and power expenditures to carry out intelligent operations locally without continuously depending on cloud infrastructure is the main goal of edge AI resource management.

Edge device middleware needs to be small, modular, and able to make inferences in real time with little overhead. Model offloading, in which more complex parts of the neural network are only run in the cloud when necessary, and dynamic inference, in which simpler models are employed when connectivity or energy resources are scarce, are two examples of energy-saving techniques.

Additional strategies include the employing of energy-efficient microcontrollers such as ARM Cortex-M series CPUs, selective sensor activation, and battery-aware task scheduling. Real-time operating systems and edge AI middleware frequently interact to handle latency-sensitive applications while guaranteeing that power limitations are met.

Optimized Scheduling for Energy-Efficient AI Workloads

Scheduling is crucial in optimizing the efficiency of AI workloads in utilizing computational resources. As deep learning training, real-time speculation, and data processing become increasingly large and complicated, scheduling algorithms must optimize for both performance and throughput, as well as energy efficiency. A sophisticated scheduler inside the middleware stack can markedly decrease total energy consumption by synchronizing tasks with available resources, decreasing idle periods, and diminishing data transfer. We examine essential solutions for energy-conscious scheduling in contemporary AI systems.

Prioritization of Tasks Based on Energy and Timelines

AI workloads frequently exhibit a combination of traits—some are sensitive to latency, whilst others exhibit more tolerance for latency Middleware-level scheduling must account for both task deadlines and anticipated energy usage to facilitate informed allocation decisions.

Energy-aware service-level agreements (SLAs) may be instituted, wherein AI applications stipulate permissible thresholds for latency or performance decline in return for energy conservation. Middleware understands these SLAs and schedules jobs accordingly, dynamically altering task priority to optimize power consumption while adhering to business requirements.

Techniques for Gang Scheduling

In AI model training and extensive simulation activities, certain jobs consist of several interdependent subtasks that must be executed concurrently across various nodes or devices. Conventional scheduling methods may isolate these subtasks, resulting in underutilization or synchronization inefficiencies. Gang scheduling addresses this issue by guaranteeing each of the subtasks of a project are scheduled concurrently as a cohesive unit.

From an energy efficiency perspective, gang scheduling minimizes idle periods when one segment of a distributed task is prepared but is hindered by another segment that has not yet been scheduled. By reducing synchronization delays and coordinating execution windows, the framework prevents superfluous power consumption resulting from incomplete activity.

In a distributed training context employing parameter servers and many worker nodes, concurrently arranging all workers and the parameter server optimizes the use of network bandwidth, CPU/GPU cores, and cache. This method yields expedited convergence, reduced inefficiencies, and diminished energy expenditures overall.

Data-Informed Scheduling

Contemporary AI workloads are data-intensive, frequently necessitating the retrieval, transfer, and processing of substantial information across memory tiers and networked storage systems. A frequently neglected contributor to energy usage in AI systems is data transfer. Data-aware scheduling mitigates this issue by optimizing scheduling decisions to minimize both the distance and regularity of data transfers.

This strategy entails positioning AI tasks in proximity to the requisite data or co-locating them alongside the pertinent storage systems. For instance, if a job regularly retrieves a specific dataset located on a designated node, allocating it to a compute node inside the same rack mitigates costly inter-network data transfers.

Data-aware scheduling considers caching solutions as well. Reutilizing a node from a cache that contains a dataset for related processes reduces both latency and consumption of energy. Middleware with data locality knowledge may monitor data placement and formulate appropriate job placement strategies accordingly.

Heterogeneous Job Scheduling Artificial intelligence systems increasingly comprise heterogeneous assets, comprising CPUs, GPUs, TPUs, FPGAs, and specialized processors. Each component possesses a distinct energy-performance profile. Effective scheduling in this context requires allocating the appropriate task to the suitable hardware according to its computing requirements and energy consumption.

A substantial matrix multiplication operation may execute most efficiently on a GPU because of its parallel architecture, whereas a control-flow-intensive task may be more appropriately handled by a CPU. Middleware systems utilizing hardware-aware profiling can autonomously align workloads with their least energy-efficient processing units.

Furthermore, energy-aware bin-packing algorithms can enhance job allocation among heterogeneous nodes by taking into account power limitations, temperature profiles, and workload attributes. These strategies avert situations in which all resource-intensive processes are concentrated on a single node, necessitating excessive cooling or throttles, thereby resulting in energy wastage.

Reinforcement Learning for Dynamic Scheduling

Conventional rule-based scheduling systems, although efficient in static settings, find it challenging to adjust to dynamic and unexpected AI workloads. Reinforcement Learning serves as an effective mechanism for adaptive scheduling, enabling middleware to acquire optimal scheduling policies by ongoing interaction with the surroundings.

In reinforcement learning-based schedulers, an agent monitors system parameters, including the length of the queue, power consumption, job success rates, and resource utilization, and selects scheduling actions such as task placement and priority adjustment. Gradually, the agent discerns which activities result in minimal energy use while preserving satisfactory performance.

A practical illustration is a reinforcement learning scheduler that adapts job timings according to real-time electricity pricing fluctuations. By synchronizing high-energy jobs with intervals of low-cost or renewable energy accessibility, the system conserves electricity and diminishes operational expenses.

Furthermore, RL-based schedulers can identify intricate patterns and nonlinear correlations between jobs and system activity that manual heuristics fail to recognize. This yields enhanced long-term energy efficiency, especially in extensive data centers and cloud AI systems.

For instance, in a research study involving a simulated data center, an RL-based scheduler was trained to allocate virtual machines (VMs) to physical servers in a way that minimized energy usage without violating service-level agreements (SLAs). The RL agent learned to predict when workloads would spike or drop and preemptively consolidated VMs during idle periods, allowing unused servers to power down. Compared to static or greedy algorithms, the RL scheduler achieved up to 20% reduction in energy consumption while maintaining workload performance.

Energy-efficient scheduling is fundamental to middleware-level optimization in AI systems. By integrating methodologies like task prioritization, gang scheduling, data awareness, heterogeneous resource mapping, and adaptive learning via reinforcement, middleware can markedly diminish the power consumption of AI workloads while maintaining performance integrity. These advanced schedulers enhance contemporary AI, increasing efficiency and promoting sustainability in innovation. Although much of this part emphasises strategies to lower energy use, it's also crucial to understand that bad scheduling choices can cause significant energy inefficiencies such as extended idle times or regular resource thrashing without providing any observable performance improvements. Sometimes, this can waste precious power resources and compromise system responsiveness.

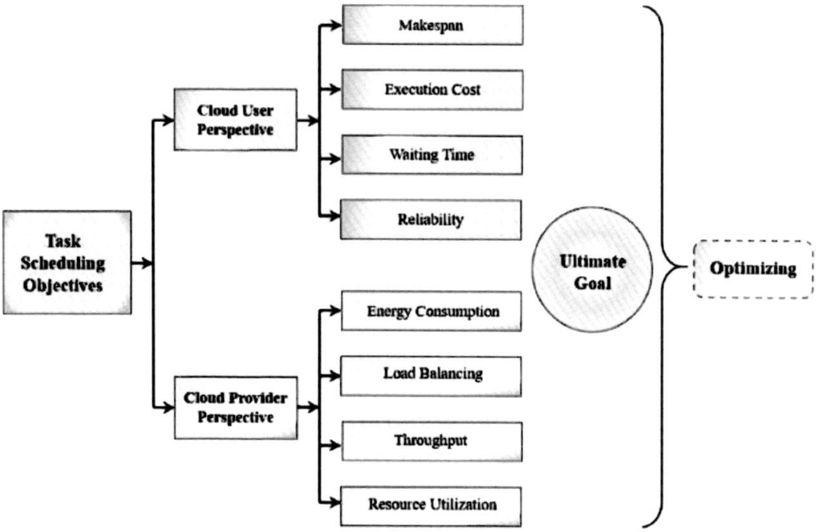

Source

Data Deduplication and Compression

AI workloads frequently need the storage and processing of redundant or closely analogous data, especially in activities such as picture classification, natural language processing databases, and model checkpoints. Data deduplication is a method that detects and removes redundancies, enabling the system to retain a singular instance of duplicated information and reference it as required. This diminishes total storage use, accelerates I/O operations, and minimizes energy-intensive data transmission.

For instance, training datasets utilized in various experiments may be uploaded periodically in distinct files or versions. Middleware-level deduplication algorithms can autonomously identify identical blocks of data or byte sequences, hence removing superfluous copies. This is particularly advantageous in shared databases along with distributed file networks, where superfluous duplication results in heightened read/write cycles and energy consumption.

Data compression, conversely, diminishes the physical dimensions of data through more effective encoding. Utilizing lossless algorithms such as LZ4 and Zstandard, or domain-specific approaches for picture and audio compression, diminishes data volume, hence reducing energy expenses through reduced disk operations and expedited transmission durations. In extensive AI implementations, minor compression improvements can result in significant energy savings, particularly when information is stored on SSDs or is often accessed throughout training and inference.

Middleware platforms that incorporate compression and deduplication at the database layer, or as part of model checkpointing, provide a robust basis for energy-efficient AI pipelines.

Strategies for Tiered Storage and Placement

AI systems manage data with differing significance, access frequency, and performance criteria. Tiered storage denotes a hierarchical storage methodology that allocates data among various storage media according to their access attributes. High-velocity, high-capacity storage such as NVMe SSDs or RAM is utilized for hot data, whilst cooler data is transferred to lower-energy storage solutions like magnetic disks or tape drives.

Middleware utilizing sophisticated data placement algorithms persistently observes access patterns and autonomously relocates data throughout storage tiers. For example, ongoing training datasets may be stored on SSDs, whilst older logs or model versions could be transferred to HDDs or cloud archive storage. This equilibrium guarantees that high-power devices remain inactive for infrequently requested data, thus conserving energy.

Cache Management and Data Prefetching

Caching is a prevalent approach employed to diminish information access latency and avoid repeated storage reads. Nonetheless, it also contributes substantially to energy efficiency. Middleware systems can circumvent repeated access to slower, more energy-intensive storage media by retaining frequently requested data in rapid-access, low-energy memory like DRAM or L3 CPU caches.

AI workloads, particularly those that entail repetitive training or batched inference, frequently access identical data repeatedly. Caching solutions guarantee that this data is preserved in high-speed memory throughout iterations, minimizing energy expenditure on I/O operations. Strategies like Least Recently Used and Most Frequently Used policies facilitate the intelligent management of constrained cache space.

Simultaneously, data prefetching predicts the forthcoming data blocks required and loads them into memory prior to their request. For instance, in the successive processing of video frames or audio samples, prefetching the subsequent set of inputs mitigates latency and energy surges caused by on-demand access. When effectively executed, prefetching can save idle CPU cycles and enhance energy efficiency, particularly on edge devices with limited power resources.

To optimize their effectiveness, caching and prefetching have to be calibrated to the specific attributes of the AI workloads they support. Middleware systems frequently incorporate adjustable policies that optimize cache size, refresh rates, and anticipation intensity to achieve certain performance and power objectives.

In-Memory Databases

Conventional disk-based databases can be energy-intensive due to frequent disk access and protracted query processing. Conversely, in-memory databases retain all data in RAM, significantly diminishing access time and energy expenditure related to disk I/O. For AI applications necessitating real-time utilization of datasets such as recommendation systems, fraud detection mechanisms, or autonomous navigation, IMDBs present a compelling energy-efficient option.

In-memory databases mitigate disk read delay, hence decreasing the CPU cycles required for data retrieval and enabling a greater number of operations to be executed per watt of energy expended. Widely utilized in-memory technologies such as Redis, Memcached, and Apache Ignite serve as rapid data layers between AI models and sluggish backend systems, providing enhanced performance with reduced power consumption.

Middleware can coordinate these in-memory technologies to enhance AI workloads further. For instance, during training, datasets or parameters for models may be temporarily stored in IMDBs, facilitating rapid epoch cycles and reducing energy consumption associated with accessing SSDs or networked devices. In inference scenarios, sustaining a rolling cache of former user interactions or input in memory facilitates rapid response times while markedly decreasing energy expenditure for each query.

Furthermore, IMDB provides meticulous oversight of data eviction, replication, and clustering, enabling middleware to grow AI pipelines efficiently with regard to power consumption.

Data management is an essential, if frequently undervalued, mechanism for enhancing the power efficiency of AI systems. Middleware can diminish I/O operations, enhance memory utilization, and lessen superfluous data transfer through deduplication, compression, tiered storage, intelligent caching, prefetching, and in-memory information techniques. When implemented comprehensively, these innovations establish a path for data that is both more efficient and considerably more environmentally sustainable, harmonizing AI advancement with the increasing demand for ecological responsibility.

Energy-Conscious Virtualization for Artificial Intelligence

Virtualization has become essential to contemporary computing infrastructure, facilitating effective resource utilization, task segregation, and scalable AI implementations. Nonetheless, virtualization can incur overhead if not engineered with energy economy as a priority. Middleware systems must progress beyond mere hardware abstraction; they must now integrate energy-awareness into the deployment, management, and decommissioning of virtual machines, containers, and serverless instances. Virtualization may substantially enhance environmentally sustainable AI systems through lightweight technologies, live migration, adaptive scalability, and more intelligent runtime environments.

Lightweight Virtualization Technologies

Conventional virtualization, dependent on hypervisors for hardware emulation, offers robust separation but is resource-intensive. Lightweight virtualization approaches such as containers, unikernels, and microVMs provide superior performance-to-energy ratios for AI workloads, particularly in microservices and transient tasks.

In contrast to virtual machines, containers utilize the host operating system's kernel, significantly minimizing boot time, memory consumption, and system calls. This optimized execution diminishes CPU cycles and decreases power consumption per task. Containers may be rapidly initiated or terminated, rendering them optimal for scaling AI applications according to demand without maintaining inactive resources in operation.

Advanced technologies such as unikernels, which integrate application code and essential OS capabilities into a singular binary, further diminish energy consumption by removing superfluous kernel elements. These ultra-lightweight devices can rapidly perform AI inference tasks and promptly shut down thereafter, conserving both energy and bandwidth in memory.

Middleware platforms enhance efficiency by providing a superior abstraction layer, particularly crucial in edge computing and high-density AI implementations.

Virtual Machine Live Migration for Optimization

In extensive AI workloads or applications deployed in cloud computing platforms, VM real-time migration is an effective method that facilitates the transfer of virtual machines to physical servers without incurring downtime. This capacity is particularly pertinent for energy conservation when utilized to aggregate workloads during periods of low demand.

Live migration facilitates thermal balancing by reallocating workloads from overheated or inefficient servers, thereby sustaining performance and minimizing the activation of fans or cooling systems. Through effective orchestration, middleware may automate choices according to utilization, energy costs, and performance metrics, resulting in an intelligent infrastructure that adjusts to energy limitations.

Dynamic Virtual Machine Scaling

AI workloads are frequently erratic, varying according to user input, training cycles, or real-time inference requirements. Facilitating dynamic VM scaling is essential for energy optimization, guaranteeing that resources are provided as needed rather than in a fixed manner.

Middleware platforms like OpenStack, VMware vSphere, and cloud-native APIs facilitate vertical scaling and horizontal scaling. By adaptively reacting to workload metrics, such as CPU/GPU utilization, queue length, or inference delay, platforms can allocate or deallocate resources in real time.

For instance, in the first stages of a batch AI training job, additional VMs may be allocated, subsequently diminished as the data loading and evaluation phases commence. This reduces power consumption during low-intensity stages while preserving speed when necessary. Integrating this with renewable-aware scheduling, escalating operations when solar or wind energy is accessible, introduces an additional dimension of sustainability.

Dynamic scaling minimizes the necessity for overprovisioning, hence decreasing idle resources that consume standby power. Through strategic scaling, AI implementations can attain optimal provisioning, synchronizing energy use with real demand.

Containerization for Artificial Intelligence

Although virtual machines are crucial for robust isolation and legacy programs, containers have emerged as the favored approach for hosting AI applications owing to their rapidity, efficiency, and portability. Containerization platforms like Docker, Kubernetes, and Podman provide efficient environments that are ideal for energy-conscious computing.

Containers facilitate resource capping by enforcing restrictions on memory, CPU, and GPU usage, preventing applications from excessively devouring power. Kubernetes's Vertical Pod Autoscaler and Horizontal Pod Autoscaler can autonomously adjust the size or quantity of containers according to workload metrics, optimizing energy expenditure to essential areas alone.

In multi-tenant setups, containers facilitate bin packing by efficiently allocating workloads to optimize utilization across fewer nodes.

Consolidating AI microservices onto fewer physical machines allows for the deactivation of the energy-saving mode of idle hardware. Moreover, container orchestration systems can emphasize energy-efficient node scheduling by utilizing cost-aware or green-energy-aware modules.

Another energy benefit of containers is that they are compatible with multi-architecture configurations, facilitating the utilization of low-power CPUs in inference deployments, particularly in mobile and edge AI contexts.

Considerations for Serverless Computing

The progression of virtualization culminates in serverless computing, referred to as Function-as-a-Service. In serverless settings, developers create and deploy AI functions without overseeing infrastructure, since middleware platforms automatically manage capacity provisioning, execution, and scaling.

This model is intrinsically energy-efficient. Serverless functions are event-driven and transient; they utilize resources solely during their execution. In contrast to perpetual services or persistent virtual machines, serverless operations remain dormant when not utilized, resulting in significant energy conservation.

A serverless function conducting sentiment analysis on fresh client reviews may execute for only a few seconds per minute. In conventional deployments, a container or virtual machine remains operational continuously for this sporadic work. Serverless architecture completely eradicates this inefficiency.

Nonetheless, serverless computing necessitates meticulous design to prevent cold start latency from impairing performance, particularly in real-time AI applications. Enhancing code for rapid initialization, employing lightweight frameworks, and utilizing provided concurrency helps alleviate these difficulties while preserving energy efficiency.

In conclusion, energy-efficient virtualization is essential for sustained artificial intelligence. By adopting lightweight virtualization, facilitating live VM migration, executing dynamic scaling, and employing containers and serverless activities, middleware can significantly diminish the energy consumption of AI workloads. These methodologies enable programmers and infrastructure teams to construct scalable, efficient, and environmentally sustainable AI systems that conform to contemporary efficiency and sustainability objectives.

Energy-Efficient Containerization for Artificial Intelligence

As AI applications expand and progress, the demand for adaptable, flexible, and efficient deployment settings increases. Containers have been a favored solution owing to their lightweight characteristics, flexibility, and ease of orchestration. In addition to operational benefits, containers offer a distinctive opportunity to enhance energy efficiency in AI infrastructure. Containerization serves as a fundamental component in developing sustainable AI systems by minimizing overhead, maximizing resource use, and facilitating precise control over workloads. Middleware that incorporates energy-efficient solutions for container setup can assist enterprises in attaining both performance and sustainability objectives.

Optimization of Container Images for Size and Dependency Reduction

Container pictures frequently comprise superfluous layers, redundant libraries, and excessive dependencies, all of which augment image size, retrieval duration, and resource use. Enhancing energy efficiency through the optimization of container pictures is a simple yet effective approach.

Reduced image sizes result in expedited startup times, diminished data transmission over the network, and decreased disk I/O, all contributing to energy conservation. Developers can accomplish this by:

- Utilizing simple base images such as Alpine Linux.
- Eliminating development tools, documentation, and superfluous packages.
- Integrating layers during the construction phase to prevent redundancy.
- Employing multi-stage builds to distinguish between build-time and runtime contexts.

For AI workloads, this encompasses optimizing model files, eliminating superfluous components of libraries such as TensorFlow or PyTorch, and incorporating the necessary inference scripts. A streamlined container initiates rapidly, operates with little RAM and CPU usage, and results in a reduced carbon footprint.

Resource Constraints and Surveillance for Containers

A significant element of container technologies such as Docker and Kubernetes is the capacity to establish resource constraints for CPU, memory, and GPU utilization. In the absence of such limits, containers may utilize excessive resources even when unnecessary.

Middleware can impose stringent constraints and demands to guarantee that containers function within specified parameters. For instance:

- Restricting an inference container to utilize a single CPU core and 512MB of RAM.
- Allocating GPU fractions to simultaneous tasks via Nvidia's device plugin for Kubernetes.
- Avoiding memory leaks that result in superfluous paging and disk I/O.

In addition to constraints, real-time monitoring is essential. Middleware systems can monitor container-specific data, including usage, power consumption, and temperature. Instruments like as Prometheus, Grafana, and cAdvisor enable operators to identify inefficient containers and implement corrective measures, such as throttling, rescheduling, or terminating idle instances. This establishes a feedback loop in which energy use is not merely restricted but proactively enhanced.

Orchestration Tools for Energy-Efficient Container Management

Container orchestration technologies oversee the lifespan of containers across clusters. These platforms include an extensive array of capabilities that can be utilized for energy-conscious scheduling, scalability, and task allocation.

A cluster may comprise a combination of high-efficiency ARM nodes and conventional x86 servers. The scheduler can allocate low-priority or inference-intensive AI containers to ARM nodes, thus minimizing total energy consumption.

Microservices Architecture for Modular and Scalable Artificial Intelligence Systems

Implementing a microservices architecture—where each AI function is divided into autonomous, containerized units—improves modularity and energy efficiency. Instead of operating monolithic applications continuously, microservices provide the targeted execution of only essential components.

Microservices facilitate horizontal scaling at the service tier. Instead of replicating the full usage, only the high-demand components, such as sentiment analysis, are scaled to optimize efficiency. Middleware that comprehends inter-service connectivity and power profiles can optimize deployment techniques to minimize redundant workloads and overlaps.

Security Considerations for Containerized Artificial Intelligence Applications

Although energy efficiency is vital, security serves a supplementary function by mitigating resource misuse, which can substantially escalate energy usage. Misconfigured or compromised containers might deplete energy by executing unauthorized programs, mining cryptocurrency, or establishing infinite loops.

In conclusion, energy-efficient containerization integrates technological optimization with strategic coordination. By reducing picture size and limiting resource consumption, as well as employing intelligent scheduling and microservices, containers provide unparalleled adaptability for developing low-power AI systems. With robust, intelligent middleware, containerized AI systems achieve agility, scalability, and environmental responsibility, thereby facilitating the advancement of sustainable computing.

Chapter 4: Frameworks for Energy-Efficient AI

Machine learning programs rely heavily on AI frameworks for their development, deployment, and optimization processes. In giving developers organised settings, they play a crucial role in efficiently creating complex algorithms. With features like distributed training, automated differentiation, and graph execution, popular frameworks like Scikit-learn, TensorFlow, and PyTorch simplify AI development. Reducing AI's energy consumption has risen to the status of a top priority, necessitating a fresh look at the role that software frameworks play in this area.

Due to their outsized impact on AI model power consumption, runtime efficiency, and computing demands, software framework optimisation for energy efficiency is of the utmost importance. Effective optimisation of frameworks can significantly cut down on superfluous processing, lessen data transit, and maximise resource utilisation. Reduced energy demands of complicated algorithms can assist in lessening their environmental effect, operational expenses, and the difficulty of making AI accessible to a wider audience. Methods such as model quantisation, pruning, adaptive training techniques, and efficient data handling inside frameworks are useful tools in this effort.

In this chapter, we will take a deep dive into different AI frameworks that are designed to be energy efficient. We will focus on practical approaches and advanced optimisation techniques that can help you achieve significant energy savings without sacrificing performance.

Topics covered in this chapter will include federated learning environments, deep learning frameworks (e.g., TensorFlow and PyTorch), distributed MLlib, and model compression techniques. In addition, this chapter will discuss optimisation tactics at the algorithmic and framework levels, illustrating their effects and efficacy with case studies and real-world examples. Readers will obtain important insights about strategically using AI frameworks to promote energy-conscious AI development from this focused analysis.

Deep Learning Frameworks with Low Energy Consumption

Using XLA Compiler with TensorFlow

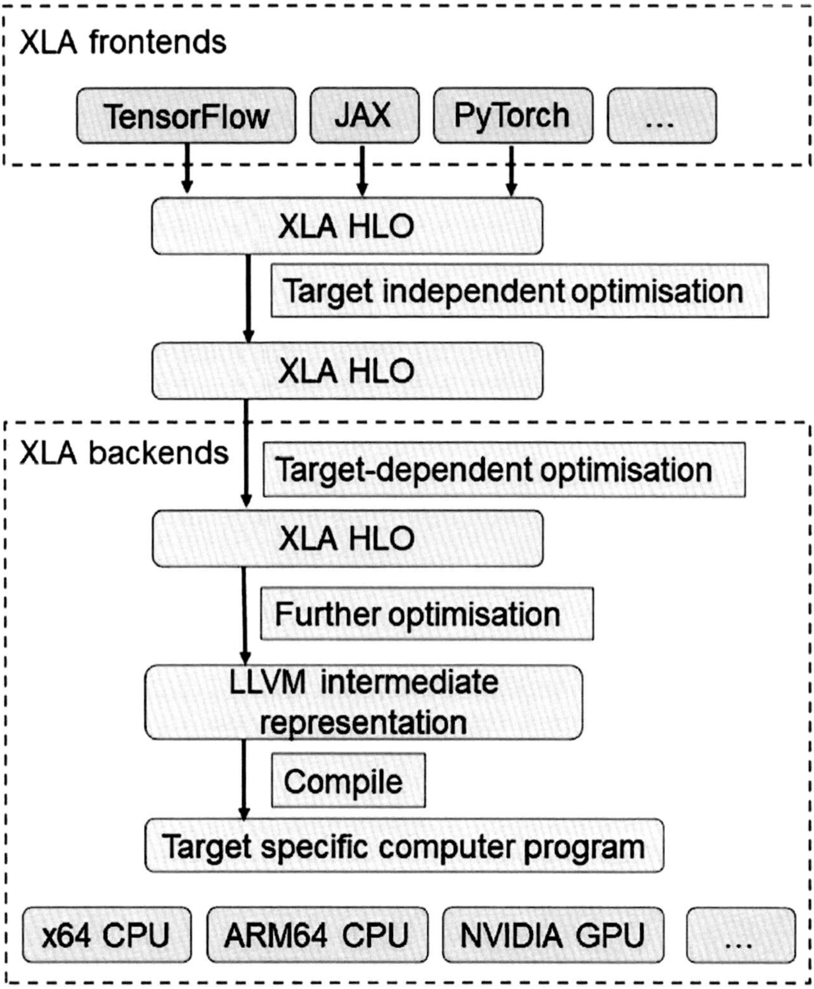
XLA frontends
TensorFlow
JAX
PyTorch
...
XLA HLO
Target independent optimisation
XLA HLO
XLA backends
Target-dependent optimisation
XLA HLO
Further optimisation
LLVM intermediate representation
Compile
Target specific computer program
x64 CPU
ARM64 CPU
NVIDIA GPU
...

Source

The open-source library TensorFlow, created by the Google Brain team, is widely recognised as a leading deep learning framework. Its strength, adaptability, and extensive toolkit make it ideal for creating sophisticated machine learning models. TensorFlow facilitates the fast construction and deployment of complex neural networks by developers.

An important development in TensorFlow, the Accelerated Linear Algebra compiler seeks to reduce power consumption and improve computing efficiency. By consolidating numerous processes into a smaller number of computational kernels, XLA improves performance and drastically decreases overhead in computational graph optimization. To minimise data movement, optimise memory use, and minimise redundant computations, XLA converts high-level TensorFlow graphs to machine code that is optimised for the underlying hardware. This simplified procedure has a direct effect on AI systems' power efficiency because it increases processing speeds, decreases latency, and decreases power consumption.

It is well-established that XLA is beneficial for graph optimisation. Reduced energy demands are a direct result of XLA's successful operation consolidation, which improves cache locality, optimises parallelisation, and decreases instruction overhead. These benefits are often shown in practical situations. Consider Google's internal use of TensorFlow with XLA; they were able to significantly lower compute latency and energy usage for language models used in production. Also, using XLA compilation instead of the normal execution modes has reduced power utilisation and runtime for convolutional neural networks used for computer vision tasks by as much as 20-30%. These examples show how XLA may improve

TensorFlow, making it an essential tool for long-term AI deployment sustainability.

JIT Compiler and PyTorch Software

Facebook's AI Research created PyTorch, and it's become very popular because of its user-friendly interface and strong integration with dynamic computational graphs. Natural language processing and reinforcement learning are two areas that are always changing, and their dynamic nature makes it easier to deal with varied input sizes and adaptive model designs.

The Just-In-Time compiler is a notable feature that greatly improves PyTorch's processing performance. To take advantage of both dynamic computation's simplicity and static graph execution's speed gains, the JIT compiler converts PyTorch models into optimised intermediate representations. By using just-in-time, PyTorch is able to translate Python code at a high level into low-level instructions that are optimised for particular hardware architectures. This process reduces overhead, processing time, and power consumption.

Energy efficiency is significantly impacted by JIT compilation. When compared to models run in ordinary interpreted mode, JIT-compiled PyTorch models frequently show execution improvements of 20-50%, according to comparative studies. Lowering the total environmental footprint of deep learning processes is achieved by a direct correlation between reduced computing time and reduced power usage. The empirical study of RNN and transformer-based models, which are frequently employed in natural language processing applications, has shown that JIT compilation significantly enhances runtime productivity and energy savings without sacrificing accuracy or performance.

The efficacy of JIT is further demonstrated by its real-world applications. When deploying large-scale NLP models like RoBERTa, FAIR made heavy use of PyTorch-JIT, which allowed for faster inference times and lower CPU loads in production environments. In real-world AI applications, these experiences highlight PyTorch-JIT's power as a tool for optimising performance and energy efficiency.

Refining and Quantifying the Model

Crucial methods used to improve deep learning models' energy economy include quantisation and pruning. When doing calculations or adjusting model parameters, quantisation is used to decrease the numerical accuracy, usually from 32-bit floating-point values to 8-bit integers or other lower-bit representations. Without sacrificing much in the way of model fidelity, this technique drastically cuts down on the computational burden, memory footprint, and total power usage of neural network operations.

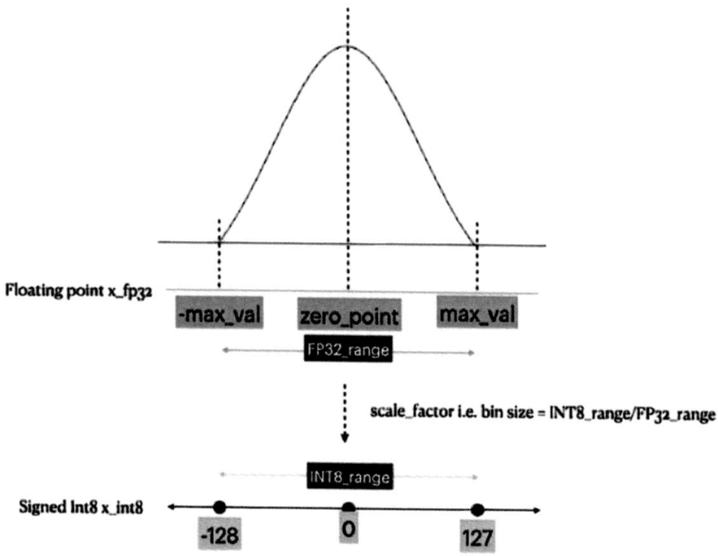

Source

Pruning, in contrast, is a method for optimising neural network architecture by methodically removing weights that are neither necessary nor helpful. Reduced computational complexity, memory needs, and energy utilisation during training and inference are all results of pruning, which removes unneeded components.

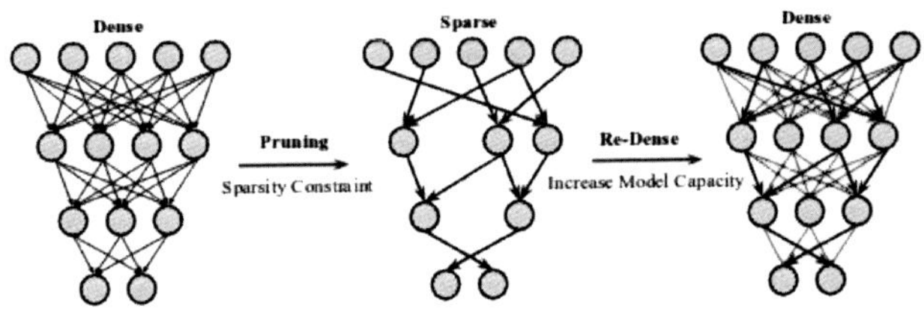

Figure 1: Dense-Sparse-Dense Training Flow. The sparse training regularizes the model, and the final dense training restores the pruned weights (red), increasing the model capacity without overfitting.

source

Strategic planning is necessary for the efficient implementation of these techniques. Quantization techniques, such as quantization-aware training and post-training quantization, are available and can be used depending on the situation. Rapid energy reductions are possible by post-training quantisation, which directly transforms taught algorithms into lower-precision formats requiring little retraining. On the other hand, quantisation-aware training entails adjusting models during retraining or fine-tuning to explicitly take decreased precision into consideration. This approach typically results in better accuracy retention while using much less power. While quantization and pruning significantly reduce model size and power consumption, they often come with a trade-off in accuracy. Quantization-aware training helps minimize this loss, but a slight performance dip may still occur. Balancing energy efficiency with model precision remains a key challenge, especially in edge deployments where both factors are critical.

Structured pruning involves deleting individual neurons or channels, magnitude-based pruning involves decreasing weights depending on their sizes, and iterative pruning and fine-tuning involve repeatedly minimizing and retraining the model. Computational complexity has been dramatically reduced in practical deployments, with transformer models and CNNs frequently reaching sparsity levels of over 50% without noticeable accuracy losses. Quantisation and pruning have a revolutionary effect in developing eco-friendly AI systems, since empirical assessments indicate energy reductions of 20% to 60%.

Strategies for Distributed Training

By distributing the training of deep learning models across several computers, we can drastically cut down on the time and energy needed to train them. In this field, data parallelism and model parallelism are the two most used paradigms.

By distributing the model among numerous processors, each of which handles a separate portion of the data, data parallelism is achieved. All of the nodes' gradients are added together. By focusing on sharing gradients instead of model parameters, this approach reduces communication cost. In contrast, model parallelism involves using numerous processing nodes to handle different parts of one neural network model, such as different layers or parameters. Very huge models, which surpass the memory constraints of individual computing units, benefit greatly from model parallelism.

Efficient communication mechanisms are essential for both paradigms to minimise energy usage. Specialised protocols like NCCL and MPI are utilised for this purpose. By enhancing the flow of data between dispersed nodes, these collective communication libraries drastically cut down on data transmission overhead, resulting in greater efficiency. By reducing idle times and making the most of hardware utilisation, energy efficiency is further improved by efficient communication scheduling, gradient compression, and asynchronous updates.

The numerous real-world examples demonstrate the practical benefits of these strategies. As an example, OpenAI trained GPT-3 and GPT-4, two large-scale transformer models, using efficient communication protocols and considerable model parallelism. When compared to conventional single-node training configurations, these methods significantly cut down on training time and energy consumption. In a similar vein, Facebook trained massive picture-classification models using distributed data parallelism, which reduced training times and energy consumption by distributing tasks efficiently across thousands of GPUs.

Finally, deep learning operations become much more energy efficient when training is done in a distributed fashion and supported by clever communication methods and parallel execution methodologies.

Machine Learning Frameworks with Low Energy Consumption

Optimisation using Scikit-learn

The open-source machine learning library scikit-learn is well-known for being efficient, flexible, and easy to use with Python. Machine learning tasks such as classification, regression, clustering, reducing dimensionality, and model selection are made available to users. Researchers, teachers, and machine learning practitioners alike have flocked to Scikit-learn for its easy accessibility and thorough documentation, which facilitates quick model building and deployment.

Dimensionality reduction approaches, which greatly simplify the dataset before training, are another successful optimisation approach. Examples include Principal Component Analysis and feature extraction methods. By doing so, we improve the model's interpretability while simultaneously decreasing the training time, memory utilisation, and energy consumption. Memory overhead and energy cost can be significantly reduced by using incremental learning procedures. These tactics entail training models in batches or streaming scenarios.

The optimisations' efficacy has been repeatedly shown by use cases and benchmarks. For instance, as compared to baseline models, researchers who used PCA in conjunction with optimised Random Forests on massive amounts of sensor data from IoT gadgets saw a 30% decrease in training time and energy consumption. Similarly, incremental learning approaches have greatly reduced power consumption for edge devices, which is especially advantageous in real-time analytics scenarios. These examples highlight the significance and practical advantages of using Scikit-learn's algorithmic optimisation approaches to produce significant gains in energy efficiency.

Distributed ML with Spark MLlib

Distributed machine learning made easy with Apache Spark's MLlib, an engine for processing large amounts of data that's both scalable and robust. Clustering, classification, regression, and collaborative filtering are just a few of the large-scale data processing and analytics tasks covered by its array of algorithms. By dividing computations among numerous computer nodes, MLlib's distributed computing architecture efficiently handles large datasets, outperforming and outscaling existing methods that rely on a single node.

The inherent energy efficiency benefits of distributed computing architectures are enormous. Spark MLlib has a direct effect on the total energy consumption of large-scale information analysis by drastically reducing computing time by parallelising machine learning workloads. Data partitioning, handling memory, and caching are all aspects of MLlib implementations that require strategic considerations in order to achieve maximum energy efficiency.

Reducing unnecessary data moves and recomputation, two major energy wasters in distributed systems, is possible with efficient data partitioning and caching solutions in Spark MLlib. Spark's in-built caching algorithms reduce disc operations and network traffic, which significantly reduces energy consumption, by storing frequently retrieved intermediate results in memory.

Optimising hardware resource utilisation and, by extension, energy usage, is possible through setting Spark's parallelism parameters, which include changing executor and core allocations per node. There are noticeable improvements in practical implementations. For instance, large-scale logistic regression models developed on cluster environments using optimised Spark MLlib configurations have reduced runtime by 40%, which is directly correlated with significant energy savings in comparison with non-optimized configurations.

These real-world examples show how Spark MLlib's strategic optimisation techniques—like data locality optimisations, efficient caching, and careful resource tuning—greatly improve energy efficiency in DL workflows that are distributed.

Engineering and Feature Selection

When it comes to optimising machine learning pipelines, the energy efficiency is directly affected by feature selection and engineering. By eliminating irrelevant, redundant, or noisy data points, feature selection systematically chooses a subset of useful features from a big dataset. Training times, computational burden, memory utilisation, and energy usage are all drastically cut with feature selection because it simplifies and minimises the dimensionality of data.

There are a few common approaches to feature selection. Some examples of filter methods are the chi-squared test and correlation analysis. Recursive feature removal and wrapper methods are examples of wrapper methods. LASSO regularisation is an example of an embedding method. You can save a lot of energy by using these approaches efficiently. As an example, filtering high-dimensional datasets to just include the top 10% of features can often decrease training times by half and power consumption by half as well.

Feature engineering is the process of improving model performance with little computing expense by adding or changing features. The core of feature engineering includes techniques such as aggregation, encoding, discretisation, and normalisation. Machine learning professionals can greatly simplify computational operations by carefully crafting these changes. As an example, one-hot encoding of categorical variables can lead to a significant increase in dimensionality and processing demands; thus, more energy-efficient methods such as aim encoding or embedding solutions may be available.

These benefits are illustrated by real-life instances. Optimal feature selection in conjunction with efficient encoding techniques reduced runtime and energy usage by 25-40% in comparison to unoptimised scenarios in e-commerce recommendation systems. These comparisons show how selecting features and engineering methods drastically cut down on computational complexity and energy usage in ML workloads.

Optimising Hyperparameters

The process of optimising algorithm-specific parameters that impact model learning and performance is known as hyperparameter optimisation. Machine learning activities' energy usage, runtime performance, and computational efficiency are all directly impacted by these characteristics. When hyperparameters are fine-tuned, models are guaranteed to have optimal configurations, cutting down on energy-wasteful computations.

Grid search, Bayesian optimisation, and random search are common approaches for optimising hyperparameters. For smaller parameter spaces, grid search is a good fit, but it can be computationally costly because it examines all possible combinations of parameters. However, overall energy consumption is reduced by random search since it examines parameter spaces randomly and typically requires fewer evaluations. Optimal configurations are frequently reached more quickly using Bayesian optimisation, which uses probabilistic modelling to systematically investigate interesting variable spaces based on past evaluations.

Hyperparameter adjustment results in significant energy savings, as demonstrated by real-world experiences. According to a comprehensive study that included large-scale neural networks and ensemble models, Bayesian optimisation saved computing effort by up to 50% compared to grid search and consistently produced better model accuracy with fewer trials. Similarly, randomised searches provide substantial energy savings compared to exhaustive grid techniques while still properly balancing exploration and efficiency.

One example is a proactive upkeep scenario that uses manufacturing equipment sensor data. Bayesian optimisation was found to be more effective than exhaustive methods in achieving optimal model configurations with half the computational resources used, leading to significantly lower overall energy demands.

The significance of careful parameter tuning in creating efficient and sustainable AI systems is emphasised by the fact that strategic hyperparameter optimisation, especially using Bayesian optimisation and randomised searches, is crucial for attaining significant energy savings in machine learning workflows.

Frameworks for Distributed AI that Consider Energy Use

Collaborative Education

Multiple devices work together to train a model using federated learning, a decentralized machine learning approach, although they do not share any raw data. For sensitive applications like healthcare, banking, and personalised advice, this technique offers significant privacy advantages. User data confidentiality is maintained, and the demand for centralised data storage is reduced by federated learning, which leverages data from numerous edge devices.

When compared to conventional centralised training, federated learning significantly reduces communication expenses and power consumption, making it more energy efficient. Federated learning transfers just the parameters of the model or gradients rather than forwarding huge data sets to a central server, which drastically reduces network traffic and energy consumption. The edge devices train locally and report back to the coordinator at regular intervals. This significantly lessens the computational resources required for dispersed training on a wide scale, as well as the bandwidth and latency of communications.

These energy advantages are clearly demonstrated by practical use cases. One example is how Gboard, Google's predictive keyboard, used federated learning on handheld gadgets to decrease energy consumption and data transmission volumes in comparison to server-based models. To further illustrate the point, consider the healthcare industry. With federated learning, hospitals may pool their patient data stored locally to train diagnostic models, drastically cutting down on energy consumption compared to centralised data processing. These examples show how federated learning can save a lot of energy without compromising privacy or data sovereignty.

Architectures for Parameter Servers

For large-scale training projects in particular, parameter server designs are the foundation of many decentralised AI systems. Here, a central server keeps track of the neural network model's global parameters, and numerous dispersed worker nodes calculate gradients using data from different sets. In order to update the parameters of the global model, the workers periodically contact the parameter server. Particularly in data-parallel and model-parallel situations, this configuration makes it easy to manage big, distributed neural network models.

Data transfer efficiency, synchronisation frequency, and parameter aggregating methods are the main resource implications of parameter server systems. Efficient parameter servers greatly decrease the energy demands of network connections and computing by minimizing redundant computations and wasteful data exchanges. Sparse communication, gradient compression, and asynchronous updates are some of the techniques that further improve energy efficiency by reducing communication costs and idle computation cycles.

Implementations in the real world show significant improvements in efficiency. Parameter servers are widely used by Tencent and Alibaba for training large-scale AI models in recommendation systems. This has led to substantial improvements in training times and energy consumption. The importance of optimised parameter server setups in attaining sustainable AI practices is demonstrated by the approximately 40% reduction in energy expenditures in these circumstances as compared to naive distributed training approaches.

Libraries for Collaborative Communication

Distributed artificial intelligence relies heavily on collective communication libraries that facilitate effective management of communication among computing nodes, such as Message Passing Interface (MPI) and NVIDIA's Collective Communications Library (NCCL). For essential communication patterns such as broadcast, reduce, scatter, and all-to-all exchanges, these libraries offer optimised procedures. Their meticulous application greatly affects the distributed training's energy efficiency.

For optimal data sharing in multi-GPU configurations, NCCL was tailor-made for GPU-accelerated computing environments. By utilising collective operations optimised for GPU technology, NCCL drastically decreases latency and bandwidth utilisation, hence minimising energy consumption linked to data transmission. However, MPI is a communication library that is optimised for a wide range of uses outside AI workloads; it is extensively used in distributed computing spanning several hardware platforms.

Research shows that there are significant variations in energy efficiency. NCCL achieves up to 25% lower energy utilisation owing to optimised GPU-aware communications and regularly outperforms MPI in deep learning workloads that focus on graphics processing units (GPUs). In contrast, MPI is more efficient and has more flexibility when it comes to CPU-bound workloads, particularly in the old-school HPC setting.

One example is the significant improvement in runtime and energy consumption observed when evaluating large-scale transformer models utilising NCCL-based protocols for communications compared to traditional MPI-based implementations. The importance of optimised communication libraries in attaining distributed AI systems with low energy consumption is demonstrated by these empirical findings.

Distributing Work and Balancing Demands

Sustainable distributed AI relies on efficient job distribution and load balancing. The goal of these methods is to avoid energy-wasteful situations in which some nodes are overburdened while others sit idle by spreading out compute workloads uniformly across all available resources. Distributed AI workflows can reduce their energy footprint with proper load balancing, which guarantees optimal utilisation of computer resources.

To accomplish energy-aware job allocation, multiple approaches have surfaced. The most efficient distribution of computational tasks is guaranteed by methods like resource-aware task partitioning, adaptable scheduling algorithms, and dynamic workload prediction, which take into account both the current workload and the availability of resources in real time. By making proper use of machine learning models and past performance data, predictive techniques improve scheduling efficacy while drastically cutting down on needless computing overhead.

Dynamic scheduling, in which jobs are distributed adaptively during execution, and static scheduling, in which jobs are distributed in advance according to anticipated resource availability, are two ways of load balancing. Particularly in heterogeneous computing systems, dynamic load balancing can lead to significant energy savings despite being computationally more demanding due to its higher responsiveness to changing conditions.

These tactics are reinforced by real-life instances. Distributed recommendation systems used by companies like Amazon and Netflix use complex load balancing strategies to reduce computing overhead and energy consumption in response to changing customer demands. Recent studies on distributed deep learning technologies have provided more evidence that these methods work. When contrasted to static, non-adaptive scheduling, dynamic task allocation with anticipatory resource management can reduce total energy consumption by as much as 35%.

Collective communication libraries, optimised parameter servers, federated learning, and strategic load balancing are all part of power-aware distributed AI frameworks that offer effective solutions to the problem of energy consumption in AI systems running on a wide scale. Organisations may greatly improve the efficiency and sustainability of dispersed AI installations by incorporating these strategies properly.

AI Model Compression for Energy Efficiency

Learning Condensation

One effective method of model compression is knowledge distillation, which involves moving information from a larger, more complicated model to a smaller, more simplified one (the pupil). Distillation enables high accuracy while drastically lowering computational complexity and energy consumption by directing smaller models to mimic the predictive behaviour of bigger, more accurate models. Deploying AI models to contexts with limited resources, such as mobile devices, edge computing platforms, or IoT devices, is where this method really shines.

The process of knowledge distillation can be broken down into several distinct phases:

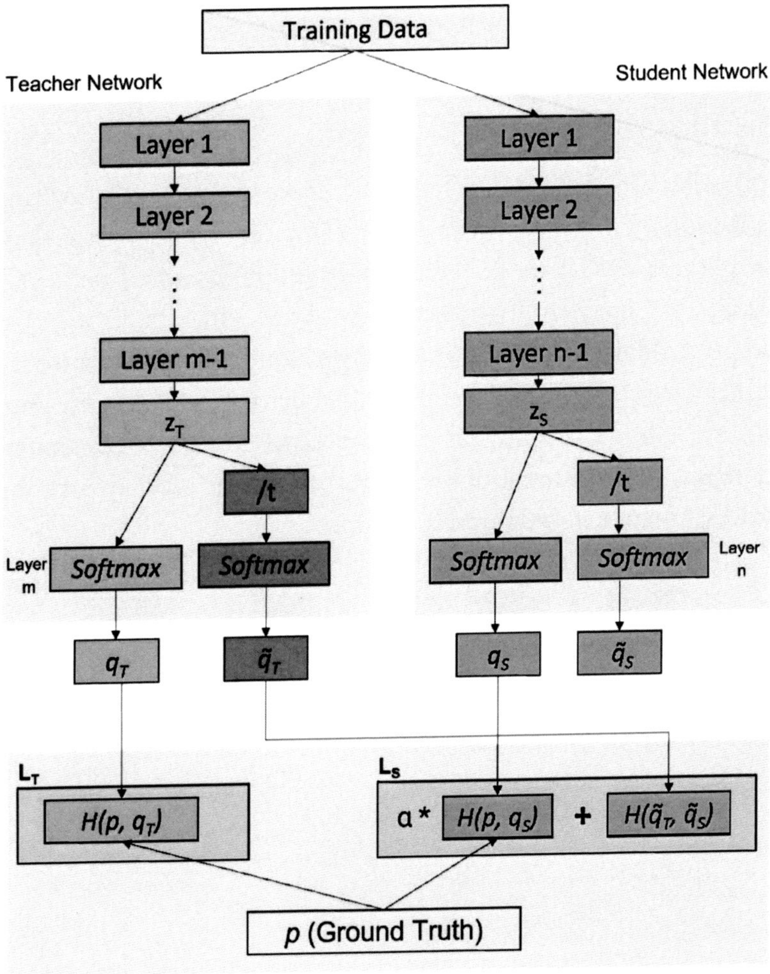

Training Data
Teacher Network
Student Network
Layer 1
Layer 2
Layer m-1
z_T
/t
Layer m
Softmax
Softmax
q_T
$\tilde{q}_T$
Layer 1
Layer 2
Layer n-1
z_S
/t
Softmax
Softmax
Layer n
q_S
$\tilde{q}_S$
L_T
$H(p, q_T)$
L_S
$\alpha * H(p, q_S) + H(\tilde{q}_T, \tilde{q}_S)$
p (Ground Truth)

Source

Initial Step: Get the Teacher Model Trained

The first step in achieving optimal accuracy is training a high-capacity model using the entire dataset.

Second Step: Choose the Student Base

A more compact and lightweight design is selected, usually with fewer layers, a lower parameter count, and lower computing complexity.

Third Step: Distillation Process

Training targets for the smaller model include both the actual labels and the softened probabilities generated by the teacher model.

In order to capture more subtle information on prediction probabilities, a temperature parameter is usually employed to smooth out the instructor model's outputs.

Fourth Step: Assessment and Implementation

A baseline model taught traditionally without distillation and the teacher model are both used to assess and compare the distilled student model.

Knowledge distillation routinely results in substantial energy and computational reductions in real-world examples. To deploy lightweight models such as MobileBERT and DistilBERT, Google used distillation techniques. These models achieved performance comparable to models based on large transformers like BERT, but with much decreased energy consumption and inference times.

Reduced computing overhead, memory utilisation, and energy consumption are proportionate outcomes of such simplified models, which display as few as half as many parameters.

Methods for Pruning

To prune a neural network model is to remove superfluous or redundant connections and parameters in a methodical way while keeping the accuracy relatively unchanged. Pruning minimises computational burdens, memory needs, and consumption of energy throughout inference and training by lowering the degree of complexity and sparseness of neural network designs.

Some methods of pruning have become more popular:

- Pruning by Measurement

Reduces the size of the network incrementally by removing weights that fall below a given magnitude threshold, frequently in an iterative fashion.

- Organised Pruning

Reduces the computational cost and memory footprint by eliminating entire neurons, filters, or layers depending on specified criteria. This dramatically improves hardware acceleration compatibility.

- Thorough Refinement by Iterative Pruning

Using iterative pruning and retraining, the model's sparsity is increased over time without sacrificing accuracy.

The significant energy efficiency gains via pruning are demonstrated in real-world case studies. To illustrate the point, Stanford researchers created a systematic pruning method called Deep Compression. It reduced parameter usage for prominent CNNs like AlexNet and VGG16 by over 90%, leading to inference speeds that were roughly three to four times faster and energy consumption that was correspondingly lower. Natural language processing systems like transformers have also shown similar advantages, with structured pruning regularly reducing computing cost and energy usage by up to 60% without compromising accuracy.

Approaches to Quantification

As a general rule, quantisation converts high-precision floating-point numbers (such as 32 bits) into lower-precision forms (such as 8-bit or 16-bit integers), thus decreasing the numerical precision of the weights, biases, and activations inside neural network models. The inference and training processes use much less energy because of this, as do the storage needs and processing demands.

One way to apply quantisation is by:

- Post-training Quantization

Changing activations and weights to a lesser level of precision following initial training with little need for fine-tuning or retraining.

Although there may be a small impact on model accuracy, this method is fast and energy efficient.

- Quantization-Aware Training(QAT)

It entails mimicking quantisation effects during training, which results in less accuracy loss than quantisation after training.

Quantisation can be applied effectively:

- If you take into consideration the intended hardware (such as mobile CPUs that enable 8-bit arithmetic) while deciding on the necessary levels of precision.

- If you need to retain a higher level of accuracy, especially in sensitive applications, you should use QAT.

- If you want to save even more energy, combine quantisation with pruning and other optimisation tactics.

Impressive outcomes are shown by real-world deployments. Using quantised neural networks extensively, Google's Tensor Processing Units achieve huge efficiency gains—a power consumption reduction of about 30-50% and a significant increase in inference throughput. Training big transformer models, like GPT-3 and GPT-4, with NVIDIA's mixed-precision quantisation (FP16) resulted in a 40% decrease in energy consumption and a considerable acceleration of training speeds.

NAS, or Neural Architecture Search

The goal of Neural Architecture Search is to automatically find the most effective neural network topologies that are optimized for a given task or hardware limitation. In order to find the best models that combine accuracy with energy efficiency, the NAS methodically searches a large search space of potential network topologies.

The usual components of NAS techniques are:

- Definition of the Search Space

In order to assess possible designs carefully, a search space is defined with a variety of network components, levels, processes, and connections.

- Methods for Finding What You Need Online

Making use of optimisation techniques based on gradients, evolutionary algorithms, or reinforcement learning to efficiently traverse this area.

- Assessment Criteria

Taking into account several goals, including precision, delay, and energy us, to direct selection towards architectures that efficiently balance trade-offs.

Methods that aim squarely at reducing energy use consist of:

NAS that is hardware-aware uses the hardware's memory footprint, computational delay, and power limitations, among other things, as part of the search criteria.
To drastically cut down on search time and computational overhead, proxy-based NAS uses low-cost efficiency predictors or substitutes to quickly estimate energy efficiency parameters while architectural selection is underway.

Some real-world applications show how NAS can cut power usage in half. Using NAS approaches that were specifically optimised for resource constraints, Google's MobileNet and EfficientNet designs were found. Despite only a fraction of the computational resources, MobileNetV3 achieved accuracy competitive with much bigger models. This allowed for high-performance inference on edge devices with restricted energy budgets. In a similar vein, EfficientNet designs routinely show substantial energy savings—lessening computational demand by as much as 80% in comparison to traditional CNN designs—all while maintaining model correctness.

Knowledge distillation, pruning, quantisation, and NAS are four ways for compressing AI models that are energy efficient. These techniques are vital for optimising neural networks to be more sustainable. By using these approaches, AI developers can drastically cut down on power usage, which improves environmental sustainability and makes it possible to deploy on renewable energy sources.

Optimising AI Models for Energy Efficiency

Closing Too Soon

In order to stop neural networks from overfitting, early stopping is a commonly used strategy that ends training when efficiency on a validation dataset starts to decline. This method drastically cuts down on training-related energy usage by doing away with superfluous computing. A model is said to have overfitted when it becomes overly specific to the data used for training, leading to ineffective generalisation and unnecessary computing burden. Models can attain optimal accuracy without increasing energy needs through excessive iterations by integrating early stopping. This improves prediction performance.

Common best practices for implementing early halting are as follows:

Step 1: Establish Metrics for Validation
To track how far along you are in the training process, use appropriate metrics like validation loss or accuracy.

Step 2: Determine the tolerance for delay
Tolerating no improvement for a certain period of epochs ("patience") before training stops.

Stage 3: Keep an eye on how well the training is going
After every iteration, compare the model's performance on the validation set.

Stage 4: End the instruction in the right way

When the validation metric shows no more significant improvement within the specified time, you should immediately stop training.

Particularly for large-scale models, studies show that early termination significantly reduces energy use. In transformer-based language models, for example, early halting can cut energy consumption by about 20-30%, which correlates with much shorter training times and less resource usage.

Scaling the Gradient

In distributed training settings, gradient compression approaches aim to minimise data interchange among dispersed nodes in order to reduce communication overhead. Because distributed training relies on each node computing its own local gradients, there is typically a lot of communication overhead due to the frequent transmission of these gradients across the network. By reducing gradients before transmission, gradient compression greatly reduces energy consumption associated with data movement and communication lag, therefore mitigating this difficulty.

When it comes to gradient compression, the two main methods are:

- Based on quantisation, applying pressure

Minimises the amount of data communicated by reducing the accuracy of gradient values.

- Using sparsification, applying pressure

Absent minor gradients that have little impact on model updates are discarded, and only a small number of substantial gradient values are sent.

These methods strike a good compromise between preserving accuracy and making communication efficient. For instance, Microsoft researchers' sparsification-based Deep Gradient Compression approach compressed gradient data by as much as 99% with almost no loss of accuracy. With energy savings of over 40% documented, this method drastically lowers computing burden, network bandwidth, and energy consumption in large-scale dispersed training.

The advantages are demonstrated by examples from the real world: Both Amazon and Facebook make heavy use of gradient compression while training suggestions and language models distributedly. This technique regularly results in significant energy savings by reducing communication overhead.

Learning Rates with Adaptation

Adaptive learning rates enhance energy efficiency and speed up convergence by dynamically adjusting step sizes throughout neural network training. Learning rates in adaptive methods such as AdaGrad, RMSProp, and Adam are adjusted for each parameter separately using previous gradient information, as opposed to the usual fixed rates. Thanks to these tweaks, convergence happens much more quickly, optimal accuracy is achieved in fewer epochs, and energy consumption drops significantly.

There are numerous real-world benefits to using adaptive methods:

- Convergence at a rapid pace: getting to the optimal level of accuracy with much less training time.

- Less computing required: Reducing computational demands and energy usage by minimizing redundant iterations.

One example is the Adam optimiser, which is commonly used for training neural networks. It routinely achieves better results in energy-efficient settings than the more conventional stochastic gradient descent. Adam achieves the requisite accuracy 30–40% faster than fixed-rate optimisers, according to comparative analyses. This directly translates to corresponding reductions in energy.

The efficacy of adaptive learning rates has been further confirmed by empirical research. The practical value of adaptive methods like Adam or RMSProp for energy-conscious training is highlighted by the consistent demonstration of substantial improvements in convergence speed and energy efficiency in deployments involving convolutional neural networks for image classification tasks, as opposed to standard SGD.

A Mixed-Precise Training Approach

In mixed precision training, neural networks are trained with lower numerical precision (usually 16-bit floating-point) for some computations that are computationally costly, and with higher precision (32-bit) for computations that are stability-critical. Mixed precision is a method for achieving high computational speeds, low memory utilisation, and high energy savings without sacrificing accuracy by deliberately combining precision levels.

The following are essential components of mixed precision training:

Controlling numerical stability means keeping certain calculations, like gradient accumulation, at a greater level of accuracy than others.

Hardware optimisation: Making use of dedicated hardware accelerators designed for lower-precision calculations, such as NVIDIA GPUs using Tensor Cores.

To avoid underflow or overflow problems caused by calculations with reduced accuracy, dynamic loss scaling automatically adjusts scale factors.

The advantages of mixed precision training are quantifiable: Ampere and Hopper, two GPUs from NVIDIA, make heavy use of mixed precision to significantly accelerate AI workloads. When compared to complete 32-bit precision training, practical deployments show a reduction of computational delay and energy utilisation of up to 50%.

The revolutionary impact of mixed precision training is demonstrated by examples of illustration of large-scale NLP models, such as OpenAI's GPT series and Google's T5, which significantly reduce training durations and power consumption. To illustrate the potential of mixed precision as a fundamental method for environmentally friendly AI training procedures, consider GPT-3 training, which heavily utilised it and achieved energy savings of 40-50% when compared to conventional precision models.

To improve AI systems' energy efficiency, we have thoroughly examined numerous optimisation techniques and frameworks in this chapter. By analysing popular deep learning and ML frameworks such as Spark MLlib, PyTorch, and TensorFlow, we have demonstrated how optimisation plays a crucial role in lowering AI's total energy consumption. A number of effective methods have evolved for model compression, including knowledge distillation, pruning, quantisation, and neural architecture search. These approaches significantly reduce computing complexity and energy consumption without compromising performance.

Additionally, it was shown that critical tactics for minimising computing requirements and consumption of energy during training and inference include model optimisation approaches such as gradient compression, mixed precision training, adaptive learning frequencies, and early stopping. In addition to facilitating faster model convergence, these approaches guarantee large energy savings, which are essential for the sustainable deployment of AI at scale.

Some emerging AI frameworks and libraries include Ray, which enables scalable and distributed AI applications, and Hugging Face's Transformers, which is known for state-of-the-art NLP models. DeepSpeed by Microsoft is also gaining traction for optimizing large-scale model training efficiently. An intriguing direction for future study and application is the incorporation of these optimisation frameworks into more comprehensive AI development plans. One surefire way to get AI solutions that are sustainable, efficient, and eco-friendly is to keep innovating AI frameworks. Developers and organisations may properly leverage the transformational potential of artificial intelligence by prioritising energy-conscious AI practices.

Chapter 5: Applications of Energy-Efficient AI

1. Introduction to AI Applications and Energy Challenges

Artificial Intelligence has swiftly evolved from a specialised field of study to an essential technology in various industries. AI applications are increasingly intricately integrated into various sectors, including healthcare, banking, agriculture, entertainment, and smart infrastructure, influencing our daily lives. Natural language processing empowers chatbots to communicate, voice assistants, and real-time translation. Recommender systems customise our social feeds and shopping experience, and robotics is revolutionising sectors from manufacturing to disaster response. The widespread advancement of AI capabilities offers significant advantages in automation, personalisation, efficiency, and insight production.

This energy requirement is not merely a technical issue; it presents significant issues for scalability, operational expenses, and environmental sustainability. The carbon impact of certain AI models is comparable to that of transcontinental flights. The dilemma is further aggravated by the trend of implementing AI on edge devices, which are limited by battery life and temperature constraints, and becoming an energy economy is an essential requirement rather than merely an ooptimization Furthermore, in areas with inadequate or unstable power infrastructure, energy-intensive AI models may become impractical or unattainable, exacerbating the digital divide.

In this setting, energy efficiency becomes a vital factor in the design and implementation of contemporary AI systems. Attaining energy efficiency necessitates a comprehensive, multi-faceted strategy encompassing hardware design, software optimisation, algorithm selection, and application-specific methodologies. Energy-aware model compression approaches, like as pruning and quantisation, can substantially diminish the computational burden during inference while maintaining accuracy. Likewise, implementing lightweight neural networks and employing adaptive execution strategies (such as early quitting or conditional computing) can enhance energy efficiency according to task complexity and resource availability.

Sustainable AI transcends a mere technological objective; it constitutes an ethical obligation. As enterprises and governments increasingly depend on AI for decision-making, automation, and innovation, it is essential to guarantee that these systems function efficiently, equitably, and with little environmental damage.

This chapter explores the practical applications of energy-efficient AI in critical areas such as computer vision, natural language processing, robotics, speech recognition, and recommendation systems. It elucidates, through technical insights and case studies, how energy-efficient tactics facilitate the development of scalable, sustainable, and inclusive AI solutions for the next generation.

2. Energy-Efficient Computer Vision Applications

Computer vision is among the most computationally demanding fields of artificial intelligence. Vision-based AI models, utilised for facial recognition in social media applications and for facilitating autonomous cars in navigating intricate surroundings, depend on deep convolutional neural networks, which analyse substantial quantities of image or video input in real time. Nonetheless, the energy expenditure of these models is considerable, especially in situations necessitating continuous surveillance, extensive installations, or edge computing. Consequently, scientists and developers have centred on enhancing vision systems for energy conservation while maintaining performance.

Efficient CNN Architectures for Classification Tasks

Conventional deep convolutional neural networks like VGG and ResNet, despite their excellent accuracy, are resource-intensive and require substantial computational power and memory. To mitigate these restrictions, lightweight CNN architectures such as MobileNet and ShuffleNet, among others, have arisen as efficient alternatives. These models are engineered to achieve high accuracy on conventional classification benchmarks while markedly decreasing the total amount of parameters and floating-point calculations.

- Depthwise separable convolutions in MobileNet split conventional convolution operations into smaller, more affordable parts. Suitable for mobile and embedded devices, this architecture preserves accuracy while significantly reducing calculations.

- Utilizing pointwise group convolution and channel shuffle operations, ShuffleNet lowers model complexity, hence allowing real-time picture categorisation on IoT devices and smartphones.

Foundational in applications like wildlife surveillance, medical image assessment in rural medical centres, and real-time categorisation on wearables, where power economy is a non-negotiable need, these lightweight devices are

Energy-Aware Object Detection: YOLO-Tiny and SSD-Lite

More computationally intensive than classification are object detection tasks, which include not just identifying objects but also finding them inside an image. On power-constrained systems, high-performance detectors such as Faster R-CNN or YOLOv4 may not be appropriate for real-time usage. Energy-efficient versions such as YOLO-Tiny and SSD-Lite have become popular to close this gap.

- YOLO-Tiny reduces the size and complexity of the original YOLO architecture, using fewer convolutional layers and smaller filters. While this leads to slightly reduced accuracy, the speed and energy efficiency gains make it highly suitable for embedded devices.

- SSD-Lite integrates depthwise separable convolutions into the SSD framework, reducing computation without sacrificing detection quality.

Widely utilised in intelligent surveillance systems, these models assume edge cameras to detect behaviours such as incursions, violations of traffic laws, or abandoned possessions in real time. Using YOLO-Tiny or SSD-Lite straight on these devices cuts down on cloud connectivity, hence greatly lowering latency, bandwidth use, and power consumption.

Efficient Video Analytics: Frame Skipping and ROI Processing

Video analytics is the continuous analysis of streams at 15 to 30 frames per second or above. Especially when the material is mostly static, examining each frame with the same intensity can result in notable energy loss. Energy-efficient video processing uses methods including:

Instead of analysing every frame, the algorithm smartly chooses important frames depending on detecting movement or scene changes. While keeping detection accuracy, this eliminates superfluous calculation.

Rather than examining the whole frame, the system concentrates on areas where action is anticipated, such as doorways in a monitoring feed or roadways in an automobile context. Non-ROI zones are either ignored completely or downsampled.

In retail footfall assessment, where energy-efficient cameras placed throughout malls or businesses record movement patterns without depleting resources, these methods are especially beneficial. They also have uses in systems monitoring traffic that call for llow-maintenancelong-term operation.

Low-Power Embedded Vision Systems for IoT and Smart Cameras

From doorbell cameras to commercial inspection drones, the growing number of edge devices has generated a great need for embedded vision systems capable of operating on low power. Often using microcontrollers or low-power CPUs with vision workload-optimized artificial intelligence accelerators, these systems.

Frameworks like TensorFlow Lite and Edge Impulse assist model quantisation and compilation methods, transforming learnt CNNs into energy-optimized binaries for microcontrollers. Custom chips such as Google's Coral TPU or Intel's Movidius Myriad X also provide hardware acceleration for vision inference with very low power envelopes, often under 1W.

Applications are:

Smart Security and Surveillance: Edge-based vision saves network traffic and energy by eliminating the need to send raw video data. For example, smart doorbells employ low-power motion detection and face recognition to activate alerts only when required.

Autonomous Vehicles and Drones use onboard computer vision to let drones track things in flight, navigate terrain, and avoid obstacles. Maximising flight time and mission success depends on using energy-efficient vision algorithms, given the short battery life of drones.

Retail Footfall Study Retail sector vision-based sensors track and categorise customers arriving or moving within a store. Often powered by batteries or solar panels, these systems can function continuously for months using minimum energy by using lightweight models and ROI-based detection.

Though with no energy-efficient solutions, its application at scale will stay constrained by power limits as computer vision develops at a dizzying speed. It is now feasible to deploy strong vision solutions within the most resource-constrained settings by combining lightweight designs, efficient detection techniques, smart processing of video, and purpose-built embedded devices. Energy-aware computer vision will be a major enabler of the AI-powered future as demand rises for intelligent visual systems from home automation to smart cities.

3. Energy-Efficient Natural Language Processing Applications

One of the most changing fields in artificial intelligence, natural language processing lets computers understand, create, and react to human language. NLP supports a wide range of applications across sectors, from translation engines and sentiment analysis tools to virtual assistants and chatbots. The energy problems are mostly caused, though, by the computational expense of training and deploying NLP models, especially transformer-based architectures. The need for energy-efficient NLP solutions gets more pressing as these models increase in size and complexity, particularly for real-time applications and execution in energy-limited settings.

Transformer Optimisations: ALBERT, TinyBERT, DistilBERT

By providing unmatched performance in activities such as language modelling, translation, and question answering, transformers have changed NLP. The models like BERT, GPT, and T5, on the other hand, are famously power-hungry, using billions of parameters and large memory footprints. Several compressed transformer versions have appeared to meet these difficulties.

Made utilising knowledge distillation, DistilBERT is a smaller, quicker, lighter version of BERT. While being 40% lighter and 60% quicker, it keeps 95% of BERT's performance on benchmark tests, hence lowering both inference and resource use.

Applying task-specific distillation and quantisation, TinyBERT pushes compression farther. TinyBERT is meant for mobile devices and edge deployment with far fewer settings.

ALBERT: A Lite BERT variant that factorises the embedding matrix and distributes parameters between layers, hence substantially lowering the amount of parameters without compromising much performance. Often, the power funds in NLP models are dominated by memory access energy; hence, this design lowers it.

The applications in which response time and energy use are important, including voice-controlled assistants in smart homes or NLP services integrated in wearables and edge devices, are most suited for these optimised models.

Energy-Aware Text Classification and Sentiment Analysis

Text classification—categorizing text into predefined labels—is a core NLP task used in spam detection, news filtering, product categorization, and more. Sentiment analysis, a subtype, identifies the emotional tone of content, such as customer feedback or social media posts.

To reduce energy consumption in these tasks:

- Shallow neural networks and optimized logistic regression models are increasingly preferred for short-text classification, where transformer-level complexity is unnecessary.

- Techniques like early exiting—where the model terminates computation early if confident in its prediction—reduce energy per inference.

- Quantized transformer models and ONNX-optimized runtimes further accelerate classification tasks on low-power devices.

Efficient Machine Translation

Because of the difficulty of modelling both grammar and semantics across languages, machine translation is among the most highly resource-intensive NLP jobs. Though they need great energy input for both training and inference, large models like Transformer-Base and Transformer-Big provide remarkable accuracy.

Energy-efficient tactics are: Model quantisation, lowering the precision of weights and activations to INT8 or potentially even lower without appreciable accuracy loss. Translation models are pruned to reduce complexity by removing superfluous attention heads and layers. Significantly lowering inference time and power draw, ONNX Runtime and TensorRT acceleration optimise model execution for particular hardware platforms.

Platforms such as Microsoft Translator and Google Translate already use such optimisations to handle billions of daily requests. More significantly, language learning systems that benefit users in low-connectivity settings can now provide excellent interpretations on mobile or offline-capable apps by integrating effective models.

Lightweight Language Models for Chatbots and Virtual Assistants

In education, healthcare, e-commerce, and customer service, chatbots are now everywhere. Maintaining these systems responsive and always-on, though, can be energy-intensive, especially when used in large-scale contact centres or integrated into battery-operated gadgets.

When task complexity is modest, lite chat agents are constructed on the foundation of TinyBERT, DistilGPT, or possibly LSTM-based architectures.

Metric	ChatGPT (GPT-3.5)	TinyBERT (Distilled BERT)	Savings/Reduction
Model Parameters	~6 billion	~14 million	~428x smaller
Inference Latency	~300-500 ms/request	~10-30 ms/request	10-50x faster
Energy per Inference	~0.5–1.0 joules/request	~0.005–0.02 joules/request	~25-200x less energy
Performance (Typical Accuracy)	~90–95% (on downstream tasks)	~85–92% (on downstream tasks)	Small reduction (3–8%)

Response generation and intent identification are distinct modules; the latter saves energy by employing smaller generative models or rule-based templates.

Common cloud-edge hybrid strategies balance latency and energy expenses by escalating complicated operations to the cloud and resolving low-level queries locally using compact models.

Its implementation has to change to be more inclusive and sustainable, as NLP shapes how people engage with machines. High-quality NLP solutions over a broad range of devices and settings are being made possible by increasing the use of energy-efficient transformer versions, runtime optimisations, and task-specific compression methods. Energy-aware NLP is paving the path for a more intelligent yet energy-responsible future, from enterprise-level translation engines to portable voice assistants.

4. Energy-Efficient Speech Recognition Applications

Modern human-computer interaction is built on speech recognition technologies. From smart home devices to accessibility tools and artificially intelligent assistants like Siri and Alexa, it allows hands-free operation and natural conversation. But, similar to other deep learning activities, automated speech recognition requires processing complicated auditory inputs, which historically calls for great computer capacity and energy. Energy-efficient voice recognition technologies are absolutely vital if these applications are to be scaled responsibly, particularly in edge devices, smartwatches, and low-power settings.

Low-Energy Acoustic Modelling

Acoustic modelling, which translates audio impulses to linguistic units including phonemes or words, is at the heart of speech recognition systems. Often combined with Gaussian Mixture Models, traditional models depended on Hidden Markov Models. Although they were light, they fell short of the accuracy required for practical use. By comparison, recent deep learning-based acoustic models like Deep Neural Networks, Convolutional Neural Networks, and Recurrent Neural Networks offer far improved accuracy but at a far greater energy cost.

Researchers have created low-energy neural acoustic models to close this gap by using temporal convolutions and depth-wise separable convolutions are used to reduce the number of parameters.

Dramatically reducing memory and computation needs by using quantised models, where weights and activations are lowered from 32-bit floating point to 8-bit integers or below. Training utilises low-rank matrix approximations to help lower the complexity of weight matrices while maintaining performance.

These optimisations produce models not only lightweight but also able to execute inference in real-time on microcontrollers and other embedded systems with low power demand.

Keyword Spotting's TinyML with Edge AI

A specialised work in speech recognition called keyword spotting, sometimes termed wake-word detection, has the system listening for a particular phrase such as "Hey Google". KWS has to be very energy-efficient to prevent battery-powered devices from being drained, as it is typically running continually.

TinyML, the area of machine learning on ultra-low-power microcontrollers, comes into play here. It's now possible to find keywords using only a few kilobytes of RAM and less than 1 milliwatt of electricity by employing optimised models like DS-CNN and TinyWakeNet.

Edge AI frameworks such as Edge Impulse and TensorFlow Lite for Microcontrollers provide tools to compress and deploy KWS models onto devices such as smartwatches, hearing aids, and IoT controllers. Operating on just one battery for months, these devices can preserve precise wake-word detection even autonomously.

Effective Pipelines for Text-to-Speech and Speech-to-Text

Full-fledged ASR systems are more than just word detection; they often also produce spoken audio from text and turn continuous voice into legible text. If not adequately optimised, both of these pipelines can be computationally heavy. These pipelines are critical in systems like real-time translators, voice-controlled devices, and navigation assistants, where performance must not come at the cost of excessive energy drain.

Applications: Smart Home Assistants, Accessibility Tools, and Wearables

A variety of interesting applications are being driven by energy-efficient speech recognition:

Wearable devices: Using KWS and small STT modules, smart earphones and watches combine voice instructions to provide subtle and hands-free control. Low-energy ASR technologies that increase battery life without sacrificing use help these gadgets greatly.

Tools for Accessibility: Voice-activated systems let those with visual or movement disabilities engage with technology using natural speech. Compact STT and TTS systems guarantee that even in disconnected or bandwidth-limited environments, accessibility features are included.

Smart Home Aides: Devices including heating and cooling systems, lights, and safety mechanisms now directly integrate voice control, utilising edge-based ASR. Constant cloud connectivity is no longer necessary, so privacy is enhanced and energy use is lowered via network use restriction.

Speech recognition's evolution is inextricable from the requirement for energy efficiency. The next stage of development will be shaped by the movement towards lightweight, optimised, and edge-compatible speech systems as voice becomes the main interface across industrial systems, consumer devices, and assistive technologies. Energy-aware speech recognition not only allows always-on and real-time capabilities but also democratises access to strong tools in settings where energy is a limited resource.

5. Energy-Efficient Robotics Applications

Robotics blends mechanical motion with smart decision-making, therefore allowing machines to carry out difficult tasks either autonomously or partially autonomously. These systems are being used more and more in many areas, including industry, healthcare, agriculture, defence, and space exploration. Still, robotics is naturally energy-hungry; it needs electricity not just for computing and control but also for mechanical actuators, communication modules, and other sensors. Energy-efficient robots are crucial to enable long-lasting, autonomous operation, especially in distant, mobile, or resource-constrained settings.

Minimal Compute Motion Planning

Motion planning is the capacity of the robot to identify a quick and safe route from one location to another. Applied in high-dimensional areas or congested settings, conventional techniques such as A*, D*, and Rapidly-exploring Random Trees (RRT) can be computationally costly.

Energy-efficient motion planning seeks to:

- Simplify models and heuristics to lower computing complexity.
- Make use of precomputed motion primitives reusable across typical navigation situations.
- Use sparse graph representations to reduce the number of necessary computations.

Some more recent algorithms also include learning-based methods, enabling robots to generalise from experience, hence lowering the requirement to calculate motion plans from scratch in comparable settings. For manufacturing floor automation, where robots do similar motions every day and may cache best motion patterns to reduce CPU consumption and energy, these strategies are particularly successful.

Sensor Fusion with Low Power for Perception and SLAM

A key feature in robotics, simultaneous localisation and mapping enables a robot to track its own position inside an unknown environment and create a map of it. Typically,y cameras, LiDAR, IMUs (Inertial Measurement Units), and ultrasonic sensors, SLAM calls for continuous sensor input.

Modern SLAM systems drastically lower bandwidth and processing needs by using event-based vision that just records pixel changes instead of complete frames.

Using simple filters like Extended Kalman Filters and particle filters with lower state dimensions, sensor fusion methods are maximised for embedded computers.

To function effectively on edge AI devices like the NVIDIA Jetson Nano or Intel Movidius CPUs, neural networks for perception are compressed using pruning and quantization.

Efficient SLAM guarantees smooth, real-time operation without overburdening battery-operated robotic arms or mobile bases in medical robotics, where high-precision navigation in limited, dynamic areas is vital, such as in remote or telesurgical systems.

Effective Pathfinding in GPS-Denied Environments

Many robotic applications take place in GPS-denied areas—underground mines, dense urban settings, underwater, or alien terrain. In such situations, robots have to navigate using onboard sensing and smart pathfinding.

In exploration robotics, such as Mars rovers, where energy is extremely limited and recharging is dependent on solar power, these strategies are absolutely essential. Energy-aware path planning here decides routes not only by shortest distance but also by energy cost, avoiding steep slopes, loose sand, or shaded places that could inhibit solar charging.

Use Cases

1. Automation of Factory Floors

Motion planning optimisations and low-power control loops help collaborative robots—cobots—work alongside people on the production line. Often relying on battery backup during grid interruptions, these robots' energy efficiency is a question of operational continuity.

2. Remote Surgery's Medical Robots

Surgical robots have to do delicate operations with little onboard resources in rural or isolated areas where energy availability is limited. While saving energy, improved SLAM and low-latency motion planning aid in keeping accuracy.

3. Exploration robots—for example, Mars Rovers

Robots working in dangerous settings or deep space have to be as energy-thrifty as possible. Every joule matters; effective pathfinding, sensor selection, and computer pipelines can significantly increase mission lifetime.

Energy-efficient computing will prove essential to opening up the next generation of autonomous systems as robotics expands its reach. Whether traversing antiseptic hospital corridors, climbing otherworldly cliffs, or welding in an industrial factory, robots have to balance intelligence with frugality. Compact hardware, clever algorithms, and energy-aware policies combined with smart technology are helping to create this balance, paving the way for a time when robots are not only able but also sustainable.

6. Energy-Efficient Recommender Systems

From tailored shopping recommendations to curated playlists for music and content feeds, recommender systems are the quiet workhorses powering the digital experiences we enjoy every day. These systems handle large volumes of data to match consumers with goods, services, or information they would probably value. The computing needs of current recommendation engines, particularly those using deep learning or large-scale collaborative filtering, can be significant. Energy economy in recommendation systems has become a crucial factor, especially for mobile-first and edge-enabled structures as user bases expand and personalisation gets more granular.

Reduced Complexity Matrix Factorization-Based Collaborative Filtering

Among the most well-liked recommendation methods is collaborative filtering. It predicts preferences by means of pattern recognition in user-item interactions, such as ratings or clicks. A major method in CF, matrix factorisation, breaks down a big user-item interaction matrix into low-rank latent components. Applied at scale, nevertheless, conventional matrix factorisation techniques might be costly in terms of computing.

To increase the energy efficiency of collaborative filtering:

Sparse matrix methods stress exclusively on observed interactions, therefore minimising pointless computation. Using alternating least squares or truncated singular value decomposition, low-rank approximations lower memory consumption and dimensionality. Instead of retraining the complete model with every new interaction, incremental updates update the model in short, energy-saving batches.

E-commerce sites, where millions of customers engage with large product catalogues, commonly apply these optimisations. Without overloading backend systems, energy-aware CF models lessen latency, save server load, and allow real-time personalisation.

Lightweight Embeddings: Energy-Aware Content-Based Models

Based on characteristics including text details, labels, or user profiles, content-based filtering suggests products comparable to those a user has liked in the past. Traditionally, these systems use neural embeddings—vectors encoding item characteristics—for similarity scoring. Large integrating tables and sophisticated similarity algorithms, on the other hand, can be energy-draining.

Lightweight embedding models like FastText or GloVe can be used instead of transformer-based encoders. Dimensionality reduction techniques compress feature vectors, reducing the memory footprint and speeding up similarity calculations. Binary hashing methods such as Locality-Sensitive Hashing convert embeddings into compact binary codes, enabling fast and energy-efficient similarity search.

This approach is effective in media streaming services, where rapid and repetitive inference is required to keep up with changing user preferences and content fluctuations.

Mobile Recommendations with Edge Inference

On-device recommendation systems are becoming more popular as users access services more and more through mobile devices. Operating straight on smartphones, tablets, or set-top boxes, these technologies eliminate the need for continuous server contact and lower network and power expenses.

Mobile-friendly policies comprise Model quantisation to INT8 or smaller formats for quick on-device execution. Reducing repeated calculation by caching regularly used recommendations. Edge inference systems such as TensorFlow Lite run personalised models locally, therefore protecting user privacy and reducing cloud energy use.

Even in locations with restricted internet access, edge recommendations on social platforms can recommend friends, movies, or posts with low latency and power use.

Maintaining scalable, adaptable, and sustainable digital services depends on energy-efficient recommender systems. Platforms may keep providing tailored experiences without paying an unreasonable energy price by combining algorithmic optimisations with effective inference frameworks. These energy-aware solutions are no longer optional but rather fundamental as recommender systems run instantaneously, on the edge, and across billions of users.

7. Quantifying AI Application Energy Footprint

Designing sustainable systems depends on knowing and measuring the energy footprint of artificial intelligence as it gets more ingrained in daily digital infrastructure. Although artificial intelligence applications provide great usefulness and efficiency, they can also be somewhat energy-hungry, especially large-scale models that do real-time inference or need regular retraining. Measuring this energy use precisely guides technical choices as well as policy plans for responsible AI growth.

Energy Benchmarks: Google Search vs. ChatGPT

Among the most surprising contrasts in this regard is the energy use disparity between a ChatGPT look-up and a conventional Google search. Estimates indicate that an individual ChatGPT query could use up to ten times more power than a usual search engine query. Although Google Search is quite performance and energy optimised, generative artificial intelligence models like ChatGPT use sophisticated transformer-based calculations spanning billions of parameters even for straightforward tasks like answering a query or finishing a phrase.

A single ChatGPT query could require as much power as running a 60W light bulb for 20 minutes, based on the size of the device and infrastructure employed. Scaled to millions of daily users, the total energy impact becomes significant. This difference emphasises the need for model optimisation and smart deployment plans to control the rising power needs of conversational artificial intelligence systems.

Estimating Energy per Inference/Training Session

AI energy consumption can be broadly divided into training energy and inference energy:

- Training sessions, especially for large models like GPT-3 or PaLM, can consume hundreds of megawatt-hours of electricity. Training a single instance of GPT-3 is estimated to require over 1,000 MWh, equivalent to the yearly energy usage of hundreds of U.S. households.

- Inference sessions are lighter per unit but occur at much higher frequency, making them a major part of the energy footprint once the model is deployed.

Estimates for small to medium models running on efficient GPUs or TPUs range from 0.1 to 10 watt-seconds (joules) per inference. These numbers multiply rapidly in high-traffic applications like social media moderation, ad targeting, or voice assistants.

Case Study: Video Generation vs. Image Generation

The disparity in energy use between AI-generated pictures and video shows how application complexity affects power requirements. Spending a model like Stable Diffusion, producing one high-resolution image might take 1 to 3 seconds of GPU time, spending roughly 200–400 watt-seconds. By comparison, producing a 10-second film with constant temporal coherence can call for either processing or interpolation of thousands of frames, usually increasing energy consumption by orders of magnitude.

This significant change emphasises the need for optimisation in content development systems and explains why energy-efficient video generation is a key study topic.

The Rise of Agentic AI Models and Energy Implications

Emerging agentic artificial intelligence models—those with long-term memory, self-initiated activity, and autonomous decision-making—represent the upcoming frontier in AI progress. Although these systems provide more functionality and flexibility, constant interaction and learning loops cause them to have far more energy needs. Multimodal processing—combining vision, text, and audio. Consistent thinking over long periods.

Deployed in fields like self-sufficient research, adaptive education, or robotics, these models' operating energy footprint might equal or surpass that of conventional computer clusters, hence generating fresh sustainability issues.

Measuring artificial intelligence's energy use is about responsibility and foresight, not only about figures. Knowing the energy profile of various artificial intelligence activities helps engineers, designers, and legislators to empower them to strike a balance between invention. Energy openness has to be a guiding factor in the design and implementation of artificial intelligence as it spreads into every area of contemporary life.

8. Summary and Future Outlook

Emphasising how sustainability may be woven into the very fabric of contemporary intelligent systems, this chapter investigated the wide range of energy-efficient AI applications. The need for smarter, more sustainable artificial intelligence has never been more pressing or more attainable from lightweight CNNs in machine vision to condensed transformer models in NLP, from energy-thrifty voice recognition pipelines to optimised robots and recommender systems.

Developers in e-commerce, healthcare, smart cities, and space exploration are progressively using techniques such as model quantisation, pruning, efficient memory access, edge inference, and energy-aware scheduling to lower computational and energy loads. These methods reduce data centre running costs and carbon footprints in addition to extending the lifespan of batteries in embedded and mobile gadgets.

The developing order of application-aware energy profiling, the technique of assessing and optimising AI energy use depending on particular job, device, and deployment context, is a key enabler of advancement in this field. This strategy promotes more complex trade-offs between power use, latency, and accuracy.

But building scalable and sustainable artificial intelligence needs for cooperation throughout the whole AI ecosystem, more than just technological improvement. To create solutions holistically, developers must cooperate closely with systems engineers, algorithm researchers, and hardware designers. Standards, funding, and instructional programs help policy makers and corporate leaders motivate energy-aware design as well.

The vision is obvious going forward: a world where artificial intelligence stays strong and widespread but also responsibly constructed, energy-efficient, and universally available. The world has to become sustainable as well as smart, as it gets more intelligent. Embedding energy efficiency into artificial intelligence's DNA will help to guarantee that its advantages touch everyone without depleting the Earth.

Chapter 6: Algorithms for Energy-Efficient AI

Starting Point with AI Algorithm Efficiency

The energy and environmental effects of artificial intelligence have, in recent times, faced criticism with the increasing usage of AI in modern systems, including mobiles and data centers. Algorithms also play a crucial or even a more significant part in energy usage management, though hardware technologies like neuromorphic circuits, application-specific AI accelerators, and low-power GPUs have gained immense popularity. All artificial intelligence processes, whether training deep neural networks or performing inference in real time on edge devices, are founded on algorithms. Processing resources being squandered, higher latency, and high power drain can stem from even the most advanced technology being made suboptimal by suboptimal algorithms.

Software-level improvements are one key weapon in the battle for greener AI. In the majority of instances, algorithmic optimisations will be capable of being used more rapidly and with greater flexibility than hardware optimisations, which occasionally require great investments and physical alterations. Writers can achieve great reductions in energy consumption without altering the hardware by enhancing reasoning and procedures governing AI models. When hardware upgrades are not feasible, as they usually are not in resource-limited environments such as mobile computing or embedded systems, this is all the more valuable. In addition, advances in algorithms can extend the application of energy-efficient computing to legacy systems, so it will have a larger impact overall.

This chapter explores other algorithmic approaches in more detail, emphasizing their contribution to the creation of long-term AI systems. We provide an in-depth overview of optimisations at the algorithmic level, such as energy-efficient training and inference algorithms, smart model selection, hyperparameter optimisation, and data augmentation. Algorithm optimization is going to be essential as AI increases in scale. This applies both to performance and the responsible development of AI within the limitations of our planet's energy resources.

Energy-Saving Training Algorithms

Training is one of the most energy-consuming aspects of the life of an AI model. It may take days, if not weeks, of training time and a great deal of energy and computing resources to construct big models such as transformers or deep convolutional networks. However, with algorithmic innovation in training methodologies, new prospects have opened to significantly improve energy efficiency without compromise on performance. Optimal gradient descent techniques, regularisation techniques, transfer and curriculum learning, and optimal training practice in training models are the four primary topics discussed in this section, which tries to enhance training efficiency.

Stochastic Gradient Descent (SGD) Updates 2.1

To train AI, Stochastic Gradient Descent is commonly employed. Although it's efficient and simple, vanilla SGD can experience slow convergence in high-dimensional or non-convex optimization spaces. As a reaction, numerous enhancements have been introduced to accelerate the convergence process, thereby reducing the number of training epochs and total energy consumption.

To make the updates more stable, momentum-based SGD adds the direction of the previous gradient to a velocity term. Especially in cost surface ravines, this reduces oscillation and improves convergence speed. To further speed up learning, a very sophisticated version named Nesterov Accelerated Gradient anticipates the next position and adjusts the gradient direction.

Adaptive optimizers like RMSProp and Adam incorporate gradient knowledge of previous iterations in order to dynamically alter the learning rate of every parameter. When controlling learning that way, the model is able to converge faster to minima as well as iteratively with fewer steps. Net energy can be saved because the time training will go down, even when those algorithms actually use somewhat more memory.

Cutting down on training epochs in deep networks by 40-60% using Adam relative to vanilla SGD directly translates into energy savings in GPU/TPU-based setups, as research suggests. It is thus an environmentally conscious choice to use clever optimisers and not just an optimisation decision.

Regularisation techniques (2.2)

Even if fast convergence is essential, this should not be through the loss of generalisation. Without performance improvement in reality, overfitting makes energy consumption explode due to unnecessary model complexity and retraining iterations. Regularisation techniques work around this by simplifying models, hence reducing the amount of work in terms of computational corrections and retraining.

Neurons are disabled randomly during training by employing dropout, a common regularisation method. In this way, to avoid overfitting, the network learns redundant representations. From the point of energy, dropout temporarily reduces the number of active computations, and as a consequence, it provides slight but appreciable energy savings per iteration, particularly when training.

Heavy weights impose penalties when L1 or L2 regularisation is applied. To compress the model and make it compute faster, L1 induces sparsity, and to make optimisation more robust and minimise re-training requirements, L2 smoothes the change in weights. It does not take much computational cost to implement these approaches, but they contribute significantly to training stability and long-term energy efficiency.

Another developing area called energy-aware regularisation goes further in that it includes energy consumption within the loss function. To take an example, the model can be pushed in the direction of lower-energy setups during training by imposing penalties on parameters or layers that cost a lot of energy.

Coursework and Knowledge Transfer

Presentation of data while training could also influence power consumption. Learning a curriculum is simulated based on human education systems, which entail transitioning from basic to advanced instances. Convergence could be sped up by training the models on simpler or more regular samples first. This enables the model to learn underlying patterns before working on hard ones.

In image classification, for example, early training loss can be reduced and convergence accelerated by training on central, high-contrast images prior to proceeding with noisy or rotated examples. Using this approach, the model can "learn how to learn," reducing the number of epochs required for training and the energy consumed.

By using pre-trained models on new, related tasks, transfer learning makes efficiency even greater. Think about the potential of adapting a convolutional neural network trained on ImageNet to execute certain medical imaging tasks. The training requirements decrease a lot—sometimes even over 90%—since only the final layers need retraining.

Based on case studies in computer vision and natural language processing, transfer learning can reduce training energy expenditure by as much as 80% compared to being trained from scratch. For example, by leveraging transfer learning, Google's BERT can be fine-tuned on minute datasets in hours rather than days, with a substantial lowering of compute and power costs.

Frameworks and Practices for Good Training

Training methods and procedures have a significant impact on energy usage, apart from algorithmic decisions. One of the fundamental practices is to alter weights after viewing a subset of data instead of an individual example or the entire dataset. This strikes a balance between the convergence of the model and the efficiency of computation, which accelerates training and is more hardware-friendly.

Shuffling the data prevents the model from learning spurious patterns from the initial organization of the data. Minimize the risk of having to retrain your model as it performed poorly on fresh data by employing shuffled batches, which enhance generalisation.

For effective scaling, parallelism during training is necessary, whether data parallelism (splitting data across devices) or model parallelism. Distributed training is possible across many GPUs or nodes using frameworks like Horovod or built-in support in TensorFlow and PyTorch. Increasing training speed and reducing energy consumption, effective distribution of the workload reduces idle time.

Notably, checkpointing stores the model state at regular intervals throughout training per training run on lengthy jobs on clusters.

PyTorch torch.utils.benchmark and TensorFlow Profiler are two framework-level energy optimisation tools that developers may use to discover inefficiencies, useless processes, or poorly optimized layers. These discoveries open the door for more efficient training loop design with less computational and power demand.

Together, these approaches form a powerful arsenal for reducing the energy load on resources during the training of AI models. Sustainability of AI depends on efficient training, which involves optimizing mathematical operations, employing smart frameworks, and reusing knowledge for jobs. These approaches must be applied for ethical and economic development when models get larger, not as nice-to-have add-ons.

Power-Saving Inference Methods

With time, most of the energy is used in inference, i.e., executing trained models to make predictions, as opposed to training massive AI models, which takes a lot of energy. Artificial intelligence models are run dozens to millions of times a day, especially in production environments like smart home devices, autonomous cars, cloud APIs, and mobile apps. Creating sustainable AI systems means optimizing inference for energy efficiency. Here, we discuss some algorithmic approaches and methods that can significantly reduce the energy spent on inference without sacrificing accuracy or reliability.

Methods for Model Compression

By employing model compression techniques, which reduce the size and computational complexity of a model, inference energy can be considerably decreased. In this context, pruning, quantisation, and low-rank approximation are the three pillars.

When a network is pruned, unwanted neurons or weights are eliminated. Reducing weights is called "fine-grained pruning," and eliminating whole neurons or channels is called "structured pruning." The aim is to decrease the number of operations required for inference by inducing a more sparse network by eliminating parameters that contribute minimally to the result. In order for hardware acceleration, structured pruning is preferable as it retains matrix forms and can be efficiently parallelised.

Quantisation of 32-bit floating-point numbers into 16-bit or even 8-bit integers is just one of the ways quantisation reduces the precision of numbers involved in computations. Quantisation reduces the computational load dramatically as lower-precision computations consume less power and less memory bandwidth. Quantisation-aware training minimizes loss of accuracy, and post-training quantisation does not involve retraining.

Low-rank approximation simplifies weight matrices by breaking them up into products of lower-rank matrices. This simplification makes inference simpler by minimizing the number of parameters and multiplications required. It performs excellently on deep networks' large fully connected or convolutional layers.

The efficiency and speed improvements from these technologies are dramatic, but they come with a downside. Unless the model is calibrated correctly, deep pruning or quantisation might decrease its accuracy. However, with some adjustment, you can decrease the inference cost by 2x to 10x while maintaining the accuracy nearly unchanged.

Extracting Knowledge

Knowledge distillation is another sophisticated method for effective inference. This method entails teaching a smaller model, called the pupil, to behave like a bigger, more accurate model, called the teacher. The student model acquires knowledge about the task from both the ground-truth labels and the teacher's probabilistic predictions, which are softer outputs.

The resulting student model is normally as fast as the instructor model but smaller, faster, and more appropriate for low-power hardware. Due to this, distillation of knowledge is an excellent method for running models on low-power devices such as smartphones, wearables, or Internet of Things devices.

A variant of BERT called DistilBERT decreases inference time and power usage by 40% with a 1-2 percentage point drop in accuracy. Similarly, production environments that focus on power efficiency often make use of TinyBERT, MobileNet, and other student-tuned models.

It is reassuring to understand that knowledge distillation is model-agnostic and hence appealing as it brings to the table a universe of options in architectures and domains as wide-ranging as vision, natural language processing, speech recognition, and recommendation systems. Moreover, energy savings are usually scaled up if distillation is used in combination with trimming or quantisation.

Computing with Approximations and Adaptations

You don't have to have perfect computing precision or be constantly running your models to perform every inference task. Adaptive and approximate computing leverage this insight to save power by dynamically adjusting processing capacity based on the importance or complexity of the input.

The early exit practice is common in this field. Systems like BranchyNet have multiple exit points incorporated into them. A sample can exit early during inference if the model is completely confident in its prediction. This bypasses processing all levels for simple inputs, significantly reducing computation.

For instance, in the task of image classification, there can be secure, centred and clear image classification at an earlier layer, with unclear or noisy inputs being dealt with across the entire network. Especially in the case of real-time applications, this dynamic inference method can cut down the average inference cost cut down to 30-50%.

Adaptive computing also incorporates precision scaling. The model does not employ high-precision mathematics across the board; instead, it scales its precision in real time based on input or context. As an example, low-confidence predictions can trigger high-precision recalculation, while high-confidence predictions proceed at low precision.

With latency and power being so crucial issues in real-time and mobile environments, methods like these really come into their own. AI systems can respond faster, consume less power, and maintain reasonable performance through the removal of unnecessary computation using approximation and adaptive techniques.

Hardware-aware Optimisation

Models need to be optimised for the hardware they run on to deliver optimal inference efficiency. Hardware-aware optimisation aims to ensure that AI models operate in harmony with the memory, processing capacity, and layout of the devices that the models are being optimised for.

While designing or building models for edge devices like ARM processors, FPGAs, or Tensor Processing Units, one should make the best use of the available accelerators and avoid bottlenecks. In order to accomplish this, calculations can be reordered in the cache, one can use some operations, or modify the layers' topology.

Automatic model graph optimisation for some hardware backends is done by auto-tuning tools such as TVM, TensorRT, and XLA. Optimised machine code with minimal memory access and maximum performance is produced by these software tools during build time after they profile models.

Pre-tuned kernels by frameworks such as TFLite, OpenVINO, and ONNX Runtime for various hardware configurations make the deployment of energy-efficient models on various platforms easy.

Runtime flexibility is the second essential part. Optimising device temperature monitoring models, battery conditions, or load conditions facilitates batch size adjustment, scaling, or switching among lightweight and full-precision pathways.

Pairing theoretical power reduction to tangible outcomes, hardware-aware optimisation effectively enables AI models to be at maximum effectiveness within any deployment configuration.

Discovery and Leveraging Energy-Conscious Models

Choosing the proper model is as important as making the model's training and inference better for AI to be viable. All along, accuracy, robustness, and generalisability have been the sole priorities of model choice. However, energy efficiency has now also emerged as a vital consideration in the model selection process for artificial intelligence systems during this era of widespread adoption on platforms with limited power, like mobile phones and edge servers. Here we look at how automated machine learning, neural architecture search, and multi-objective optimisation could assist developers in finding a compromise between performance and energy consumption.

Accuracy vs. Energy trade-offs

Today, it's not as easy to evaluate a model as seeing how accurate it is or the loss. Instead, AI engineers who are energy-aware more often now view the problem as multi-objective optimisation, so they try to maximise accuracy while minimising computing cost, latency, and energy consumption. This is particularly significant when applying AI models on low-powered machines such as smartphones, drones, or Internet of Things sensors.

The Pareto frontier is an important concept in this domain; it's a line that represents the set of models in which there's a betterment of one goal at a cost of loss of the other. Optimal trade-offs are models that fall somewhere along the frontier; traversing along the line, they sacrifice some energy for increased accuracy, or conversely. This helps organisations and developers choose models that are "good enough" for their requirements without placing undue energy burdens.

As an example, a model that is 99% accurate might consume twice as much energy as one that is 97% accurate. Even with this modest gain, the extra power cost may not be justified in most real-world use cases such as content suggestions, voice commands, or spam filtering. Overfitting to data and energy budgets can be avoided by developers at the same time, using evaluation metrics that are aware of energy usage.

How to Search for Neural Architectures (NAS)?

Neural Architecture Search can automate the determination of an optimal model architecture that fulfills all the conditions, including energy efficiency, compared to the use of expert knowledge and trial and error involved when selecting an architecture by hand. If extended to include energy as a primary constraint during the search, NAS is an even more effective tool for sustainable AI development.

Traditional NAS methods required thousands of GPU-hours, which were notoriously expensive. Two newer approaches, Efficient NAS and Differentiable Architecture Search, have made NAS much more practical. ENAS reduces computation by sharing parameters among child models, while DARTS reformulates the search as an optimisation problem that can be solved continuously, making the way for speedier gradient-based approaches.

In order to make NAS systems even more energy-efficient, energy-aware algorithms incorporate metrics such as inference delay, memory access cost, floating point operations, or even true hardware energy metrics in the reward function of the search algorithm. Consequently, we have architectures that perform well on the target hardware and under the prevailing deployment conditions.

A notable success here is MnasNet, a mobile architecture that is created by NASA that surpasses hand-tuned models such as MobileNetV2 in terms of efficiency and accuracy on smartphones. Balancing latency with energy usage on devices with varied capabilities created by Facebook's ChamNet using platform-aware search.

AutoML methods

Extending NAS, Automated Machine Learning automates several processes such as data preprocessing, feature selection, model tuning, pipeline integration, and architecture selection. In the context of AI workflows that are aware of energy efficiency, contemporary AutoML tools are priceless because they have started to optimise with energy and resource constraints in mind.

To more effectively recommend models that consider time, memory, and energy constraints, resource-aware environments are now accessible in tools like Google AutoML, Auto-Sklearn, Microsoft Azure AutoML, and TPOT. Anyone wishing to deploy great AI solutions without wading through the weeds of model development will benefit greatly from these tools.

AutoML platforms usually employ evolutionary algorithms, Bayesian optimisation, or reinforcement learning to perform multi-objective searches across pipelines. Such platforms may give long-term, accurate, and scalable pipeline suggestions by incorporating energy indicators such as battery life effect and energy per inference.

A company creating a fitness smartphone app, for example, could use AutoML to discover the most energy-efficient lightweight model for step detection, one that balances reasonably well between accuracy and power usage. An intelligent camera software could also stress low-energy, low-latency models to be able to run in the background all day without heating up the device.

Hyperparameter Optimization to Increase Efficiency

Hyperparameters, such as learning rates, batch sizes, regularisation strengths, and dropout rates, are crucial to the performance of machine learning models. All can be improved with sensitive tuning to lead to better convergence, precision, and generalisability. A significant contributor to the energy budget of AI research is hyperparameter optimisation, which is computationally expensive and typically involves repeated runs of training. To developers' relief, energy-aware hyperparameter tuning is achievable now with the help of a variety of methods, making them able to reduce resource consumption without compromising performance.

Searching Methods

Searching many times over a set of hyperparameter settings is a classic technique for hyperparameter tuning, as is random search and grid search. While simple to implement, these approaches often waste resources exploring suboptimal configurations, especially with time or energy limits.

Bayesian optimisation is a better approach; it entails iteratively choosing promising configurations to evaluate next and constructing a probabilistic model of the function from hyperparameters to performance. Bayesian optimisation significantly reduces the number of training runs required by capturing uncertainty and focusing on high-potential regions. This leads to lower power consumption per optimisation iteration, which is especially evident in deep learning tasks.

Increasingly, developers are including energy usage metrics in the objective function to make these strategies energy efficient. An example is a search that would optimise for a weighted mix of accuracy and energy per training or inference cycle instead of pure accuracy or loss. Optimisation is made wiser with this multi-objective approach.

Example Case: Edge Natural Language Processing Models

Suppose a programmer is optimizing a text classification model to optimize it for use in a wearable device. Discover the best setup by using Bayesian optimization with a two-objective function: maximize accuracy and reduce inference delay and energy consumption. The model provides nearly identical performance to the baseline but with 30–40% less power consumption during inference. It does this by reducing the batch size and decreasing embedding dimensions.

It is also possible to incorporate early termination mechanisms during tuning trials. In order to save computation and energy, trial models might be terminated early if they do not perform well within the first few epochs. This method, which is also called adaptive resource allocation, keeps cycles from being wasted on configurations that are bound to fail.

Meta-Learning Methods

When it comes to hyperparameter tuning, meta-learning provides an attractive alternative to standalone search algorithms in terms of energy efficiency. Faster convergence on optimal configurations in new tasks is achieved through meta-learning, which leverages existing knowledge from earlier experiments.

Training a surrogate model to forecast the efficacy of a hyperparameter setup using past data from comparable tasks is a common meta-learning strategy. By reducing duplicate processing and narrowing the search space, this surrogate can be used to achieve faster and greener optimisation cycles.

Given structural commonality in model behavior, cross-task generalization is a specific meta-learning approach that brings optimization experience in one task to another. Hence, switching between work and datasets takes fewer training cycles.

If a research team has tuned hyperparameters for a BERT-based model on product review classification data, they can apply that knowledge to customer support chat data tuning as well. They avoid more than half of the computing cycles and energy expenditure that would otherwise be needed by starting with established hyperparameter values rather than starting from scratch.

Utilising known good configurations as a starting point for optimisation instead of taking wild guesses is another related concept. Coupled with energy-conscious loss functions and transfer learning, this allows developers to recycle optimisation knowledge in a sustainable fashion.

Optimised Data Sampling and Augmentation

High-quality training data is necessary to build robust AI models, but acquiring and preprocessing variable, giant datasets can be resource-intensive. To address this, sampling and data augmentation procedures are employed to maximise energy usage, improve generalisation, augment datasets, and reduce the need for exhaustive labelling. But not all methods of augmentation are created equal; indeed, some of them require a substantial amount of computing power. Here we consider data augmentation and sampling techniques that are less computationally hungry but still do the trick.

Inexpensive Methods of Enhancement

For data augmentation in modern AI training pipelines, especially in fields like speech recognition and computer vision, it is an important operation. It is a routine practice to generate new training examples from available data. Flipping, cropping, rotating, applying colour jitter, and scaling are usual manipulations on images. These operations consume minimal computing resources and can be performed by using GPUs or CPU pipelines with little or no power usage.

These inexpensive changes save energy through minimizing the number of training epochs required for convergence, thereby lessening overfitting. Target performance can be achieved faster with one that has been trained from a dataset with slight augmentations compared to one developed from raw, unchanged data. This can lead to savings in training energy of 20-30% in edge environments, such as when training with mobile GPUs or embedded systems.

The computational overhead of expensive augmentations like adversarial perturbations, advanced geometric warping, or neural style transfer is considerable. They are not typically energy efficient except when absolutely essential, but may increase models to be more robust in certain scenarios. Therefore, AI workflows caring about energy should have a default of a well-balanced strategy that gives precedence to cheap and efficient augmentations.

Augmenting Generative Data

Generative Adversarial Networks and other generative models are increasingly being utilized for data synthesis in cases where existing datasets are unbalanced or insufficient. In the case of under-represented classes or rare events specifically, GANs can generate high-fidelity samples that enhance the generalisability and robustness of the model.

In contrast, GAN training has been found to be highly resource-intensive, requiring special hardware and an extended training process. The question then arises: can energy-hungry augmentation be done through this process?

Reusing and using it selectively are the secrets. Light conditional GANs trained on missing classes or pre-trained generative models are alternatives to training GANs from scratch. To avoid wasting time and effort, these models can detect which classes are under-represented and generate synthetic examples for only those. Compared to full-scale training, this focused augmentation not only enhances class balance but also reduces computational expense.

One such captivating area of research is zero-shot data synthesis, which employs class descriptions rather than examples to synthesize data from pre-trained models. It has the promise to augment low-label, low-energy datasets in the near term, but it remains an evolving topic.

Active and semi-supervised learning

In building a dataset, the most expensive part is typically data labelling, which requires human effort as well as computational resources. By labelling only the most informative instances of a dataset and then selecting them, active learning reduces this burden. To maximize model performance using a few labelled instances, active learning selectively chooses valuable examples. This minimizes annotation effort and training power.

In an active learning cycle, a small labelled subset is utilized to train an initial model, and the model is then prompted to classify only those data points it is uncertain about by an oracle, like a human annotator. In some use cases, this iterative approach can make operations more efficient by up to 60% by concentrating energy spending on data of high impact.

Similarly, models can be trained on labelled as well as unlabelled data through semi-supervised learning. To decrease computational expense and human effort, methods like consistency regularisation (which imposes robust predictions under data perturbation) and pseudo-labeling (which gives labels to unlabelled data based on model predictions) exploit large amounts of unlabelled data.

Applications where one has plenty of data but no labels, such as web scraping, sensor readings, or user-generated data, are greatly helped by these methods. Active and semi-supervised learning, combined with energy-aware training methods, form a powerful strategy for the development of low-cost, sustainable AI.

Investigative Reports and Evaluation Criteria

Theoretical advances in algorithms are useful, but more concrete evidence of progress is provided by real-world case studies and benchmarks. Researchers and implementers can derive meaningful insights from comparisons between AI algorithms that consume less energy for training and inference, especially for real-world deployment. Significant benchmarks and case studies illustrating the real-world impact of energy-conscious algorithms in cloud-scale and edge environments are featured in this section.

Comparison of Vanilla and Efficient Optimisers for Training

Using the CIFAR-10 dataset, authors discovered that an Adam optimiser-trained ResNet-18 model cut GPU usage and energy consumption in half, from 90 epochs with vanilla SGD to 45 epochs. Adding learning rate scheduling and batch normalisation enhanced total energy savings by approximately 55% without necessarily decreasing accuracy much.

Another research examined BERT-based NLP models and discovered that employing DistilBERT to distil knowledge reduced training time by half and energy consumption by half, with only a 1.5% drop in performance on GLUE benchmark tasks.

Inference Performance Measures: Adaptive Execution and Compression

Quantised versions of these models, as indicated by inference benchmarking studies of MobileNet and EfficientNet, reduced latency by up to 30% and decreased power usage on ARM-based edge devices by 60-70%. Importantly, the loss in accuracy was less than 1-2%, demonstrating that precision-scaling can yield substantial energy savings without a significant trade-off.

An intelligent surveillance system deployed BranchyNet, an architecture supporting early exit routes. Without compromising detection accuracy, the model early exited for approximately 65% of input video frames, reducing computation expenses by about 40% and reducing battery consumption during real-time executions.

A Hybrid Perspective on Deployment on the Edge and in the Cloud

Edge contexts like smartwatches and drones have enabled constant execution of AI workloads with minimal battery impact using low-energy models such as compressed CNNs and TinyML variants. Example: Google's microcontroller-based keyword-spotting model consumes less than 1 mW due to tight quantisation and trimming processes.

Technology companies are applying energy-conscious scheduling and AutoML with energy constraints in cloud platforms. This has led to a reduction of 10-20% in GPU-hours on hundreds of ML pipelines.

What Lies Ahead and What Will We Face?

There is a growing necessity for robust frameworks, tools, and standards to guide the construction of energy-efficient AI. Much success has been achieved in building energy-conscious algorithms, but many challenges and outstanding questions remain. Addressing these issues is paramount if we wish to advance the field and include energy efficiency as a standard consideration in AI construction.

Creating Uniform Energy Measurements

Lack of standardised energy measures and evaluation procedures is a significant hindrance. For hardware, batch size, input form, and even ambient temperature, energy usage can change significantly, as opposed to accuracy or F1 score. Currently, there is no consistent method to compare energy usage across different models, frameworks, or hardware setups. It is not easy to come up with reliable conclusions regarding energy efficiency or compare methods fairly because of this variability.

Work is ongoing to develop energy-aware standards that can assess power usage over time, energy-delay product (EDP), or joules per inference. While nascent solutions are presented by tools like CodeCarbon, CarbonTracker, and Green Algorithms, broader consensus and integration into mainstream ML libraries are needed.

Improving Developer Tools with Energy Awareness

Energy use continues to be treated as an afterthought by developers, who emphasize optimisation in terms of latency or precision. This needs to shift so that developer-oriented platforms and tools begin to integrate energy considerations into model development. There are energy-aware optimisation flags available in the leading frameworks, including Hugging Face Transformers, TensorFlow, and PyTorch, as well as support for integrated development environments (IDEs) and real-time energy profiling boards.

The emergence of AutoML platforms that inherently consider energy constraints, proposing not only the most efficient but also the greenest models, is a promising move in the right direction.

Organisations can monitor and minimise their carbon footprints during production thanks to energy-aware models deployable at scale through embedding with MLOps platforms.

To say...

The power use of artificial intelligence is a rising concern as it scales across different companies and devices. This chapter explores methodologies that span training, inference, model selection, hyperparameter tuning, and data processing, enlightening on the integral role played by algorithms in creating AI systems that consume less energy.

Model compression, knowledge distillation, adaptive inference, and Stochastic Gradient Descent improvement can reduce inference energy, and transfer learning, regularisation, and Stochastic Gradient Descent can reduce training costs. To assist developers in attaining performance without unnecessary power consumption, the chapter highlighted techniques like smart model selection using multi-objective optimisation and hyperparameter tuning with Bayesian and meta-learning techniques. By reducing the volume and complexity of the training set, effective data augmentation and sampling also reduce energy usage.

One key lesson from these methods is the importance of integrating hardware and application layers into the algorithm design process. Optimizing software for the unique features and limitations of the base platform, whether it's a mobile processor, edge device, or cloud server, results in huge energy savings. Optimizations done at the algorithmic level are sure to translate into real-world efficiency benefits employing this holistic approach.

Green artificial intelligence must not be an add-on, but a top priority in the future. This requires encouraging collaboration among software, hardware, and system designers; integrating energy metrics into standards, benchmarks, and research methodologies; and assigning equal priority to efficiency and accuracy.

Thoughtful algorithmic design is the path to AI sustainability. Greener, more sustainable technology, where innovation and sustainability are synonymous, can be driven by the AI community through the incorporation of energy awareness at all levels of development.

Chapter 7: Future Directions and Research Ideas

Trends in Energy-Efficient AI

With the increase in size and complexity of artificial intelligence (AI) systems, the imperative for energy-efficient and sustainable AI has never been greater. The following trends, which are shaping the energy efficiency landscape of AI, provide hopeful directions for transforming intelligent systems into greener, more accessible, and eco-friendly ones.

Quantum Computing for AI

Quantum computing has turned out to be an innovative paradigm that can potentially revolutionize AI computation. Fundamentally, quantum computing uses the principles of quantum mechanics—i.e., superposition and entanglement—to handle information in radically different manners from classical computers.

The energy implications of quantum computing are complex. Quantum annealers such as those from D-Wave run at cryogenic temperatures and need a lot of power for cooling systems. Gate-model quantum computers, however—such as those built by IBM and Google—are quickly getting better in energy efficiency per operation as they scale to fault-tolerant systems.

Even with the promise, there are still huge hardware challenges. Qubits are extremely noisy and sensitive to external environmental fluctuations, so quantum error correction is a requirement, but error correction incurs overhead. Creating quantum hardware that is stable, energy-efficient, and scalable remains a core research challenge in the field.

Edge AI and Federated Learning

Another exciting trend is the move away from centralized AI models toward Edge AI, pushing intelligence onto edge devices such as smartphones, wearables, and IoT nodes. On-device inference greatly lessens the necessity for continuous data transmission back to cloud servers, which is both energy-profligate and latency-softened.

Parallel to this, Federated Learning (FL) provides decentralized training for AI models. Rather than uploading raw data to central servers, FL allows devices to locally train models and send updates on the model. This not only adds security but also saves on the energy needed to transfer data.

Applications of Edge AI and FL are growing fast. In medicine, smartwatches can do real-time diagnostics and monitoring without cloud computing. In smart cities and homes, energy-conscious AI systems can optimize appliances, heating, and lighting. In industrial IoT, edge-based anomaly detection avoids machine failure with low energy usage.

In combination, Edge AI and FL provide a key infrastructure for constructing scalable, secure, and energy-efficient AI systems within distributed environments.

Explainable AI (XAI)

With the increasing complexity of AI systems, transparency and trust in decision-making procedures become essential. Explainable AI (XAI) aims to provide transparent model predictions that are interpretable by humans. However, explainability comes with computational overhead, raising an important question: Is explainability incompatible with energy efficiency?

Not necessarily. In fact, simpler, interpretable models by nature—such as decision trees, rule-based systems, and linear models—actually use much less energy than deep neural networks. These models are not only quicker to compute but also simpler to deploy on energy-restricted platforms.

Even within deep learning, techniques for model compression (e.g., pruning, quantization) can help interpretability as well as efficiency and generate a desirable synergy. With researchers delving into surrogate models to make sense of black-box systems, keeping such surrogates lightweight and computationally thrifty becomes an increasingly strong desire.

Finally, marrying XAI with energy-conserving methods not only enables sustenance for green initiatives but also enhances user confidence, particularly in sensitive fields like medicine, finance, and law enforcement.

AI for Environmental Sustainability and Monitoring

AI is also being used to conserve the environment and maximize the use of natural resources. AI assists utilities in power forecasting by enabling them to forecast power demand and vary generation accordingly, reducing wastage and facilitating the integration of renewable sources.

In wildlife conservation, AI-based image and acoustic detection systems track endangered animals and poachers in real time. Such applications tend to use low-power sensors deployed in remote settings, so energy efficiency becomes a requirement for around-the-clock operation.

Ethical Considerations in Sustainable AI

As we progress towards efficient AI, it is essential that the transition is influenced by ethical paradigms. Energy justice is a theme that points to the need for just access to green AI technology in countries and communities. While tech giants can be optimized for efficiency, developing nations and under-resourced institutions risk being left behind.

Establishing regulatory norms and reporting mechanisms for energy consumption during AI training and deployment can reduce these risks. Public and private sectors have to collaborate to establish sharp benchmarks, invest in compute data centers powered by renewable energy sources, and give priority to models that balance performance with sustainability.

Research Challenges in Energy-Efficient AI

Although substantial progress has been achieved in optimizing artificial intelligence for energy efficiency, a few research challenges remain that constrain the broad adoption and scaling of green AI. These include benchmarking, system design, hardware-software integration, data movement, fairness, and energy-accuracy trade-offs. Overcoming them is essential to constructing AI systems that not only perform but also are sustainable and inclusive.

Lack of Standard Energy Benchmarks

Perhaps the most pressing challenge in the energy-efficient AI domain is the lack of standardized benchmarks to measure and compare energy consumption across different platforms, workloads, and environments. Unlike accuracy or speed, which are solidly quantified and well-reported, energy consumption is frequently overlooked or measured irregularly. Such transparency detracts from meaningful comparison and inhibits the pace of energy-conscious AI progress.

Existing energy reporting is very fragmented. Some research employs wall-socket power meters, while others use simulation models or resource utilization estimations. These approaches differ significantly in accuracy and are frequently non-reproducible.

To fill this gap, there is an increasing demand for standardized tools, datasets, and protocols that can yield consistent, comparable, and interpretable energy metrics. EnergyVis, CodeCarbon, and PowerAPI are such steps in the right direction, providing APIs that enable carbon emission tracking or power consumption tracking during AI training and inference. But more needs to be done towards wider adoption and integration into standard frameworks.

Industry efforts are also starting to emerge. For example, MLPerf, the MLCommons benchmark suite, has added an "Energy" category for measuring energy consumption in addition to standard performance metrics. The Green500 list ranks supercomputers based on energy efficiency instead of raw performance, promoting sustainable system design. All these notwithstanding, we still do not have AI-specific, platform-independent standards that can inform developers, researchers, and businesses to make energy-conscious decisions.

Hardware-Software Co-Optimization

Energy efficiency in AI cannot be addressed at one layer—hardware and software need tight integration. Conventional AI software stacks typically presume there will be lots of compute and memory available. But as energy becomes increasingly limiting, software needs to accommodate the capabilities and constraints of lower-level hardware.

Hardware-aware compilers are beginning to fill this gap. They can optimize machine learning workloads for particular hardware profiles, tweaking memory access, instruction pipelines, and data movement for optimal energy efficiency. Systems such as TVM and XLA (utilized in TensorFlow) are just a few instances of compiler stacks that optimize code for hardware backends, optimizing both speed and energy consumption.

Another method is code pruning—removing useless computations or network layers at model runtime, depending on the target hardware. For instance, models can avoid redundant ReLU activations or remove entire branches during inference with minimal impact on accuracy.

At the hardware side, capabilities such as Dynamic Voltage and Frequency Scaling (DVFS) enable chips to dynamically change their power consumption based on load computations. This can only work effectively when software is coded to deal smartly with the hardware's power states and scheduling algorithms.

This inter-disciplinary cooperation among chip designers, computer programmers, and artificial intelligence scientists is still in its early stages. Institutions and businesses need to create settings where these hitherto disciplined fields overlap to co-design solutions bottom-up.

Reducing Energy for Data Movement

Amazingly, data movement takes more power than computing data. Research has indicated that reading data from DRAM can use an order of magnitude more energy than a floating-point operation. This has created data movement to be one of the largest hurdles in energy-efficient AI.

To counter this, architectural advances such as near-memory processing (NMP) and in-memory computing (IMC) are on the rise. These models try to get the computation nearer to where the data is located and thus minimize energy and latency due to conventional CPU-to-memory data transfer.

On the application side, programmers can use techniques such as data reuse, memory locality optimization, and prefetching to reduce unnecessary memory accesses. Tiling methods, commonly applied in convolutional neural networks, divide operations into smaller on-chip memory fitting blocks where repeated access to the same data can occur without main memory round-trips.

Latest deep learning libraries and runtimes are starting to support these optimizations, but much more effort needs to be expended to make them available, automated, and applied to a variety of workloads and environments.

Balancing Accuracy and Efficiency

One of the principal philosophical and technical problems in energy-efficient AI is balancing model accuracy and energy use. Historically, the desire for greater accuracy has resulted in larger and more complex models. These improvements are often accompanied by high energy expenses and decreasing returns.

To counter this, researchers are looking into probabilistic computing and approximations that deliver "good enough" outputs with significantly less energy consumption. For most real-world applications—e.g., recommendation systems or alert systems based on sensors—precision to the exact is not always required, and thus approximation becomes a valid compromise.

In addition, adaptive systems that dynamically scale model complexity depending on workload or energy supply are being investigated. For example, a voice assistant can switch to a lower-precision model when in battery-saving mode without sacrificing user experience.

Developing robust frameworks for adaptive precision, early exit from inference pipelines, and context-aware model selection could dramatically enhance energy efficiency while keeping performance within acceptable bounds.

Ensuring Fairness and Equity

Energy-efficient AI solutions also need to engage with issues of algorithmic fairness and access. Increasing literature indicates that energy-optimized or compressed models tend to perform poorly on underrepresented or minority populations, leading to ethical concerns regarding the inclusivity of these solutions.

To maintain inclusivity without sacrificing efficiency, developers must make sure that energy-saving methods do not systematically benefit one demographic or data distribution over others. This means retraining or fine-tuning models on diverse datasets even after compression or pruning, and testing performance across all pertinent groups.

Community initiatives and open-source data sets can aid in this area. Projects such as AI Fairness 360 or Inclusive AI provide auditing tools and responsible deployment tools for models. Additionally, frameworks that allow developers to analyze energy vs fairness trade-offs at the model selection and training phase are also in need.

At a worldwide level, inclusive access to green AI technologies is still a significant barrier. Most low-resource areas have neither infrastructure nor investment capability to install energy-optimized systems, even though they are among the most impacted by climate change. Facilitating open research, affordable hardware options, and energy-efficient AI toolkits can narrow this gap and ensure democratized access to sustainable AI.

Promising Research Directions in Energy-Efficient AI

As artificial intelligence becomes increasingly ubiquitous in everyday life and critical infrastructure, energy efficiency needs to transform from an afterthought to a first-order design principle. Various promising research directions provide novel routes to making this happen, each based on next-generation computing paradigms, biologically inspired frameworks, and system-level integration. These strategies not only save energy but also facilitate scalable, robust, and responsive AI systems across domains.

Energy-Aware Neural Architecture Search (NAS)

Neural Architecture Search (NAS) has become a revolutionary technique for automating machine learning model design. NAS has conventionally aimed to optimize for performance metrics such as accuracy or model size. Recent developments are now propelling the field toward energy-aware NAS, where energy usage becomes an integral part of the search goal.

State-of-the-art energy-conscious NAS architectures incorporate hardware performance measurements like floating-point operations per second (FLOPs), inference latency, and explicit power consumption. In doing so, the NAS engine is able to search over a model architecture search space with energy considerations made an integral part of the cost function.

One of the areas of interest is optimizing NAS outputs for deployment on edge devices like mobile phones, wearables, or IoT sensors. These platforms have limited battery life, compute power, and thermal headroom. To solve this, energy-aware NAS not only chooses optimal layer types and kernel sizes but also restricts the architecture to fit particular hardware profiles.

For instance, scientists have shown NAS methods that produce CNNs with sub-1MB memory sizes, which allow real-time classification on microcontrollers without incurring too much loss of accuracy. These breakthroughs indicate a future where deep learning models will not only be made to work, but to work efficiently, anywhere.

Approximate and Stochastic Computing

Classic computing architectures assume that each bit of computation needs to be precise. Yet, most AI applications—particularly in vision, language, and sensor-based processing—are probabilistic in nature and can afford some imprecision. This observation is the foundation for the new areas of approximate computing and stochastic computing, which seek to sacrifice precision for energy savings.

Approximate computing targets the reduction of precision for operations, storage, and data representation on a selective basis. Rather than employing 32-bit or 64-bit floating-point numbers, low-energy models could employ 8-bit integers or even binary operations. This minimizes switching activity in circuits, memory access rate, and data transmission requirement, all leading to reduced power consumption.

Stochastic computing, in contrast, represents data as random bit streams and does arithmetic by means of basic logic gates. Although less accurate than deterministic computation, this approach significantly minimizes transistor count and energy per operation.

These algorithms have their greatest potential in image classification, where approximate predictions are often good enough for edge detection or object recognition. Likewise, sensor networks can be helped by low-resolution data gathering and processing, stretching the battery lifespan in distant or inaccessible locations.

In language modeling, stochastic sampling and low-bit quantization enable models to work well even with extreme energy limitations. Combined, approximate, and stochastic computing provide a radical reconsideration of how AI can work when energy, rather than accuracy, is the number one priority.

Neuromorphic Computing Brain-Inspired Architectures

Biological systems, especially the human brain, represent the gold standard of energy-efficient computation. The brain uses only about 20 watts—less than a light bulb—and outperforms state-of-the-art AI in flexibility, learning performance, and contextual understanding. Neuromorphic computing attempts to replicate such biological efficiency through brain-inspired devices and architectures.

At the core of neuromorphic systems are Spiking Neural Networks (SNNs), which simulate the way neurons in the brain communicate via short electrical pulses. In contrast to conventional ANNs that process on fixed time steps and continuous signals, SNNs process only when needed, making them well-suited for event-driven, sparse computing.

Neuromorphic processors like Intel's Loihi and IBM's TrueNorth have shown the promise of this method. These processors are designed for asynchronous event-based operation, with memory and processing distributed in a way that minimizes data movement and idle energy usage.

Applications for neuromorphic AI range over real-time robotics, wearable technology, and autonomous sensing networks—fields where low power and quick response are critical. Even though still under active research, neuromorphic computing is a revolutionary departure from the way we think about and develop energy-conscious AI hardware.

AI for Energy Optimization in Infrastructure

In addition to lowering its own energy consumption, AI is increasingly being used to minimize energy consumption throughout physical infrastructure such as data centers, smart grids, and renewable energy systems.

In data centers, predictive analytics powered by AI can predict server loads and allow dynamic workload balancing and cooling techniques that lower electricity consumption. AI systems can also detect underused hardware and move workloads to eliminate the energy cost per computation.

In power grids, AI assists in predicting usage patterns, identifying faults, and balancing supply and demand in real time. IoT sensors and smart meters, backed by ML algorithms, enable grid operators to control the delivery of electricity dynamically, efficiently integrating renewables and lessening dependence on fossil fuels.

In addition, green scheduling algorithms can cleverly match compute-intensive AI tasks with times of excess renewable energy availability. For instance, performing large model training during peak solar generation hours ensures that AI development does not contribute to grid stress or carbon emissions.

These uses demonstrate the promise of AI not only as an energy consumer but as a forceful actor in managing and saving it at the system level.

Energy-Efficient Robotics and Automation

Autonomous robots, drones, and autonomous vehicles demand high-performance AI to "see," "feel," and explore their surroundings. Yet, the fact that they depend on limited energy supplies—such as batteries or onboard power sources—makes energy-efficient robotics research a key frontier.

One important area is the design of low-power SLAM algorithms. SLAM is essential for real-time navigation in an unfamiliar space, but it has historically been computationally intensive. New algorithms target redundancy reduction, use light feature descriptors, and employ probabilistic techniques to reduce energy expenses without sacrificing dependability.

Real-time decision-making must also be accommodated on low-power platforms. Methods such as hierarchical planning, sensor fusion optimization, and behavior-based control enable robots to make clever decisions with low computational overhead.

Certain scientists are finding inspiration in nature to create bio-inspired robots. Such systems replicate the energy-efficient flight and locomotion mechanisms of birds, mammals, and insects and utilize actuation energy-minimizing materials and structures. In conjunction with embedded neuromorphic processors or ultra-low-power microcontrollers, such robots are capable of working for long durations in an autonomous manner, even in resource-poor or remote locations.

Powering AI Data Centers for the Future

With the continued exponential growth of artificial intelligence, the energy footprint of AI-scale compute infrastructure is becoming a concern of international urgency. Large-model training, intelligent service hosting, and real-time inference at scale demand unprecedented amounts of computational capacity, increasing electricity usage as well as carbon output.

By the end of the decade, industry reports forecast that AI workloads may account for 10–20% of global data center energy use. This growth is exerting extreme pressure on cloud vendors such as Amazon, Google, and Microsoft to move towards carbon-neutral operations. These organizations are spending significantly on renewable energy purchases, sustainable hardware design, and carbon accounting infrastructure, but extrapolating these to address AI's future needs will necessitate further innovation in energy procurement and management.

Small Modular Reactors (SMRs) as a Power Source

Among the most fascinating—and contentious—candidates to fuel next-gen AI hardware is the use of Small Modular Reactors (SMRs). These are small nuclear reactors aimed at quicker deployment, reduced capital expense, and scalable capacity over conventional nuclear power plants.

SMRs provide some benefits for data centers. They give them a consistent, low-carbon source of electricity, which is important to preserve 24/7 uptime for high-density clusters of AI workloads. As they are inherently modular, SMRs can be placed near computation centers, thereby limiting transmission loss and reliance on the grid. In principle, a single SMR might support a hyperscale data center and emit practically zero greenhouse gases.

Still, though, the mass deployment is in its nascent stages. Rollout timetables, regulatory clearances, and social acceptance are all major challenges yet to be overcome. Safety concerns persist, yet new SMR designs feature passive cooling and next-generation containment mechanisms that seek to reduce risk to a minimum. Nevertheless, vigorous debate persists on the environmental and economic costs of nuclear-powered AI infrastructure, particularly in comparison with renewables.

Renewable Energy + AI Workload Scheduling

In the short term, a more feasible solution is combining renewable energy sources—solar and wind—with smart workload scheduling. AI training tasks can be dynamically scheduled to coincide with high renewable generation hours, thus reducing dependence on fossil fuels.

Methods such as predictive load balancing, thermal storage, and AI-based job queuing allow data centers to predict renewable availability and adapt workloads accordingly. Battery storage can be utilized to balance demand during non-generation time, while smart cooling systems minimize energy consumption during peak load times.

Most promising, perhaps, is the idea of AI systems controlling their own energy profile. With real-time carbon intensity monitoring, AI models can determine when and where to train or serve inferences, scaling up during clean energy windows and scaling down during dirty grid hours. This dynamic compute scaling positions the AI pipeline as an engaged actor in the larger energy ecosystem.

Together, SMRs and renewable-aligned scheduling are two poles of a range of solutions, each with its own potential to fuel the future of AI in a cleaner, smarter, and more sustainable manner.

End Note

The quest for energy-efficient artificial intelligence is more than a technical optimization—it is a foundation of the larger effort to build a sustainable digital future. As AI continues to infuse every corner of our lives, from medicine and transportation to communication and climate monitoring, its energy footprint has emerged as a critical global issue. Yet this challenge is also an extraordinary opportunity. By rethinking how we design, deploy, and scale AI systems, we can align technological advancement with the imperatives of sustainability.

In this chapter, we have covered a broad set of trends and avenues of research ranging from neuromorphic architectures and quantum computing to energy-aware neural architecture search and low-power robotics. Combined, they show that energy-efficient AI is not an individual innovation but a product of interlinked innovations in software algorithms, hardware design, system architecture, and operation strategy.

This advance relies on something greater than engineering skill—it requires an interdisciplinary collaboration involving policymakers, ethicists, environmental scientists, and technologists. Successful solutions will need to take into account not just performance criteria and power usage, but social equity, data privacy, carbon footprint, and regulatory conformity. The future of green AI, therefore, will be constructed not just in research laboratories but in legislative chambers, classrooms, and public discourse.

By investing in energy-conscious AI today, we set the stage for a tomorrow where intelligence and sustainability go hand in hand, enabling humanity to innovate without sacrificing the health of our planet.

Verses Kindler Publication

Reach us through our website -

https://www.verseskindlerpublication.com/

For more information visit our

Instagram or Facebook page.